Colorado's

RODEO ROOTS

ROOTS

to Modern-day Cowboys

KATHRYN ORDWAY

THE
DONNING COMPANY
PUBLISHERS

The Donning Company Publishers
184 Business Park Drive, Suite 206
Virginia Beach, VA 23462

Steve Mull, General Manager
Barbara B. Buchanan, Office Manager
Pamela Koch, Editor
Dan Carr, Designer
Stephanie Danko, Imaging Artist
Mary Ellen Wheeler, Proofreader
Anne Cordray, Project Research Coordinator
Lori Kennedy, Project Research Coordinator
Scott Rule, Director of Marketing
Travis Gallup, Marketing Coordinator

Barbara A. Bolton, Project Director

Library of Congress
Cataloging-in-Publication Data

Ordway, Kathryn, 1980–
Colorado's rodeo roots to modern-day cowboys / by Kathryn Ordway.
p. cm.
Includes bibliographical references.
ISBN 1-57864-277-9 (hardcover : alk. paper)
1. Rodeos—Colorado—History. 2. Rodeos—Colorado—History—Pictorial works. I. Title.
GV1834.55.C65O73 2004
791.8'4'09788—dc22
2004013791

Printed in the United States of America by
Walsworth Publishing Company

This book is dedicated to my mother and father who gave a lot to get me to where I am today, both financially and emotionally. I would like to thank Tom Noel who found me in the right spot at the right time. I would also like to thank Emily and Meghan for their help in putting this book together and keeping me sane; they helped me more than they can ever know. A special thanks goes out to Stephanie Seifried (smseifried@hotmail.com), Mathew Staver, and Dino G. Maniatis for their wonderful photographs. I would also like to thank the staff at *Colorado Country Life* for their help in getting this project off the ground. Finally, a special thanks goes out to Kate Hunley, who mocked my comma disability but helped me out more than words can ever express.

FOREWORD *by Dr. Thomas J. Noel* *5*

INTRODUCTION *8*

COLORADO, THE BIRTHPLACE OF RODEO *17*

THE BUSINESS OF RODEO *49*

RODEO FOR THE YOUNG'UNS *65*

ALTERNATIVE COWBOYS & COWGIRLS *95*

MODERN-DAY COWS & COWPOKES *117*

CONCLUSION *149*

BIBLIOGRAPHY *157*

ABOUT THE AUTHOR *160*

FOREWORD

ONE OF AMERICA'S OLDEST SPORTS got its start in the tiny (pop. 598) town of Deer Trail on the high plains of Colorado. Deer Trail, the only town in America with that name, commemorates a path along Bijou Creek, first used by deer, buffalo, and antelope, then by stagecoaches and the Kansas Pacific Railway, which built through Deer Trail in 1869 on its way to Denver.

A railroad depot and a stockyard made Deer Trail one of Colorado's first cow towns. Large herds of longhorns driven up from Texas as well as short-horns from local ranches were driven into Deer Trail for shipment to the Kansas City stockyards. As thousands of cattle, horses, and cowboys descended on the baby cow town sixty miles east of Denver, it hosted the first United States rodeo in 1869.

The rodeo took place on July 4, one of the few holidays that cowboys enjoyed. Cowboys gathered to settle bets on who was the best rider, roper, etc. A collection of outlaw horses—beasts that were difficult or impossible to ride—was brought in. One young cowpuncher, Will Goff, boasted that he "could ride anything with hair on it." Among the contestants was a quiet Englishman by the name of Emilnie Gardenshire, who worked for the Mill Iron Outfit. He drew Montana Blizzard, a bay horse from the Hashknife.

Gardenshire climbed aboard cautiously and, once firm in his saddle, whipped the horse but kept both his hands free. For fifteen minutes, the bay bucked, pawed, and jumped from side to side before tiring out. Gardenshire then rode around the circle at a full gallop. For this magnificent piece of horsemanship, Gardenshire won the title "Champion Bronco Buster of the Plains." His prize was a new suit of clothes.

After this first rodeo, Deer Trail did not hold another one until 1912 when a rodeo and fair began to be staged annually at the Deer Trail Fair Association grounds. Some of the same fearless cowboys who staged America's first rodeo may well have been in on another Deer Trail first—a pioneer effort to start a cowboy union. Cowboys earned only twenty-five to thirty dollars a month and had to supply their own horses, saddles, and equipment. It was at Deer Trail that some of them started the Cowboys Cattle Company. This outfit, like the rodeo, made a few news stories and then disappeared. Not until 1937 would rodeo cowboys organize a union. They formed the Cowboy Turtle Association in Massachusetts after sixty-five of the top cowboys walked out of the World Championship Rodeo in the Boston Garden on November 1, 1936, to protest low prize money. So named because many cowboys felt they were late in organizing, the Turtles set dues at five dollars a year and had no initiation fee. The Turtles may have been late in organizing, but they proved to be tough. Taking advantage of the federal government's pro-labor, New Deal–era policies, the Turtles demanded better working conditions and more prize money, and they staged strikes to force rodeo producers into compliance. The Cowboy Turtle Association has evolved into today's Professional Rodeo Cowboys Association (PRCA), which has its headquarters, museum, and hall of fame in Colorado Springs. Thanks to the PRCA, rodeo is now big business. More than forty-five rodeos, including Denver's National Western Stock Show and Greeley Independence Stampede and Colorado Springs' Pikes Peak or Bust, are nationally televised each year. The PRCA sanctions nearly seven hundred rodeos in forty-seven states and four Canadian provinces.

Rodeo, which began as a little bet between a few cowboys, is now riding high. Winning rodeo riders now receive more than a new set of duds. Denver's National Western Stock Show Rodeo now features not only cowboys, but also Mexican vaqueros, cowgirls, and even little kids riding sheep in the mutton busting contests. And, like the first rodeo, these remain contests that are ultimately won by the animals, whether it takes them a few minutes or just a few seconds to get someone off their back.

In this book, Kathryn "Katy" Ordway tells the story of rodeo, then and now. Katy, a fourth-generation Coloradoan, wrote her master's thesis at the University of Colorado at Denver on this Wild West sport. She is an athlete—a triathlon competitor and a basketball player and coach. Katy, a devout rodeo fan, is a schoolteacher who is introducing her high school students to American history—and to the sport epitomizing the contributions of black, Native American, Hispanic, and gringo cowboys and cowgirls.

Tom "Dr. Colorado" Noel
Professor of History
University of Colorado at Denver

INTRODUCTION

*R*ODEO IS AN AMERICAN INSTITUTION. It is the only sport in the United States that has developed from a way of life and a way of making a living. Rodeo culture and the cowboy are seen as defining aspects of this country. Americans are described throughout the world as cowboys. When the Olympics are held, Americans walk in wearing cowboy hats. This is seen as a symbol of our country. The cowboys were one group that went west into the open spaces beyond the Mississippi River. They fought for the land, they fought through the elements and the lack of water, and they came out triumphant. While the cowboys were not the only group to be found in the West, they are the group that is most closely identified with the region. They claimed a wilderness and tamed it; the United States as a people followed the dream of Manifest Destiny. We spread from the original thirteen colonies to fill the entire continent. It is this frontier spirit that makes us who we are as Americans. In fact, one could argue that the closing of the frontier with the 1890 census was a highly traumatic event for our country that sent us searching for new frontiers. After all, frontiers are how we define ourselves. President Kennedy in the 1960s looked to the stars. In the twenty-first century, we must look to our Western past.

These two cowboys climb the fence to get a better look at the world behind the chutes at the 2004 National Western Stock Show in Denver. *Photograph by the author*

The rodeo that is in existence today consists of eight events that evolved from the skills needed to work with cattle on the range. These events are saddle bronc riding, bareback riding, steer roping, team roping, tie-down roping, steer wrestling, barrel racing for the ladies, and the most popular, bull riding. Contestants who compete in these events are scored in different ways to determine the winner of the day money and to select the champion of the entire rodeo in every event. Day money is the money that is given to the best cowboy in an

event for the day. The champion is the cowboy with the highest score or best time for the entire rodeo. The money is important for cowboys because professional cowboys gain points for every dollar they earn at a sanctioned rodeo. The more money they make, the higher their ranking.

As for the scoring of timed events, the winner is judged based upon completion time. For example, the fastest barrel racer is the winner. Timed events are the roping events and steer wrestling. These are timed through the use of gates. Time begins when a contestant breaks through the gate. It ends when the judge holds up the flag saying that a task is completed. The rough stock events—saddle bronc riding, bareback riding, and bull riding—are judged on skill. Winning riders are those with the most points who stay on their animal for the full time. Their fellow cowboys, who award points based on style, judge these men. If a cowboy draws an animal that does not buck well, he is given the option to draw a new animal to try again. This can be a risk for a cowboy, and, usually, he will weigh his options and standings before going ahead with his second chance.

Most of these events require the cowboys to draw for an animal. The rough stock riders draw for the animal they will be riding. Participants in the timed events, except for barrel racing, draw for the animal they will be tying down or wrestling to the ground. This has allowed for the development of the stock contracting industry where animals are specifically bred to make the lives of the cowboys more difficult. In fact, a few former cowboys have retired and gone on to lucrative careers as breeders. One of the best examples of this occurred in the 1930s when many former cowboys were beginning to branch out into other aspects of rodeo, which made the sport even more exciting.

Left The word "rodeo" is spelled out on a hillside in Golden, Colorado, near the junction of Sixth Avenue and I-70. It can be seen as travelers make their way into the mountains. *Photograph by Mathew Staver*

Right These tickets are from the 2004 National Western Stock Show. One is from a rodeo; the other is from the Mexican Rodeo Extravaganza, a popular cultural event. *Photograph by Mathew Staver*

Every cowboy and cowgirl understands the importance of a good pair of boots, even at a young age. *Photograph courtesy of Robert Lamb*

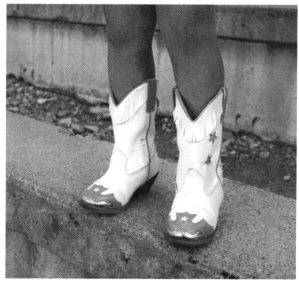

Cowboys remove their hats for the National Anthem at the 2003 Greeley Stampede. Rodeo is an American tradition dating to the late 1800s. *Photograph courtesy of Tara Roskop*

One of those was Leonard Stroud, a famous trick rider and roper, who later became a rodeo promoter. According to the *Kiowa County Press* of June 2, 1939, Stroud was just as interested in the men as in the livestock, and by the 1930s, one began to see the animals gaining importance. Famous bucking horses like Midnight and Five Minutes to Midnight began to steal any show they were a part of during their careers. These two horses were so good that both found their way into the Rodeo Hall of Fame. For the rodeo celebrating the fiftieth anniversary of Cheyenne County, Stroud and the rodeo committee of Cheyenne Wells imported a "herd of longhorn steers from old Mexico … for the steer riding and bull dogging event." Today, stock contracting is an important aspect of rodeo, and in the case of certain horses and bulls used in rough stock events, the animals often get more publicity than the riders.

As for the events themselves, what is required of the cowboy differs every time. The skills used in rodeo all come from the Old West heritage of Hispanic and Anglo-Americans and the big cattle drives of the 1800s, which

It is never too early to get started in the rodeo world. Here, a very young child gets an early taste of life on horseback before he can even walk. *Photograph courtesy of the Schowalter family*

Below left Two young cowboys are getting ready for the bull riding event at an April 2002 high school rodeo competition at the Jefferson County Fair Grounds. *Photograph courtesy of Connie J. Templeton*

Below Austin and Jordan Anderson are pictured at the 2003 Larimer County Fair and Rodeo. Austin is a calf roper; his sister Jordan was a mutton buster at this rodeo. *Photograph courtesy of Kim Anderson*

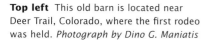

Top left This old barn is located near Deer Trail, Colorado, where the first rodeo was held. *Photograph by Dino G. Maniatis*

Top right The Deer Trail Tribune building is in the foreground with the Deer Trail water tower in the background. Today, this is a small town in eastern Colorado, located off I-70. In 1869, this was a town surrounded by cattle ranches, which made it an ideal place to hold the first rodeo. *Photograph by Dino G. Maniatis*

Center left Two children at the Elbert County Fair in August 2003 sit quietly and watch the excitement of rodeo unfold before them. *Photograph courtesy of Suni Olkjer*

Center right This steer wrestler jumps from his horse to the steer while his partner or hazer looks on from horseback at the Logan County Fair in Sterling, Colorado, in August 2003. *Photograph courtesy of Reesa Isbell*

Right A little cowboy with a big hat enjoys his first rodeo at the 2004 National Western Stock Show. Events such as the Stock Show help recapture an agricultural past that is rapidly disappearing. Today, only 1 percent of Coloradoans live on farms. *Photograph by the author*

Above Rodeo is not for the faint of heart. Here, a cowboy is thrown from his horse at the June 2000 Elizabeth Stampede, making the spectators hope he lands safely. *Photograph courtesy of Steve Diamond*

Left These cowboys are loading bulls into the chutes at the Jefferson County Fair Grounds. After the contest, these valuable animals will be put back in trailers and returned home. *Photograph by Stephanie Seifried*

A horse stands in the mud in the parking lot at the Jefferson County Fair Grounds. *Photograph by Stephanie Seifried*

Below This calf appears to be floating as the cowboy at the June 28, 2003, Greeley Stampede prepares to finish the task of tying three legs in the calf roping event. *Photograph courtesy of Pat Rains*

Above In many events, a good horse is just as important as a good rider. This girl and her stick horse look longingly at the real things. *Photograph courtesy of Judy Rush*

Below Sheep wait outside for their part in the sheepdog competition at the 2004 National Western Stock Show. The rodeo is only one of many events that take place at the large fairs held throughout the state. *Photograph by the author*

were depicted in Western films, coloring our view of our past. The roping events involve a contestant, or in the case of team roping, two contestants, capturing an animal, usually a steer or a calf. This would be done on the range to either cull the herd, that is, to remove undesirable animals from the herd, or in the case of roping, to brand a calf to prevent a valuable animal from being claimed by another outfit or by rustlers. Steer wrestling, or bull-dogging as it is sometimes called, would have been used on the range to return an animal to its rightful place.

The rough stock events have evolved for different reasons; however, the ultimate purpose was to aid cowboys in controlling the cattle. Bareback riding and saddle bronc riding were developed because cowboys needed a good horse to chase after cattle and to drive them to their ultimate destinations, and good horses were running wild in the American West. The difficulty was you had to catch one and tame it to the saddle, which was no easy task. Cowboys would try to ride these horses both bareback and with saddles in an attempt to break them to the will of humans. Once a horse was broken and trained, the cowboy was set to go. This was the real start of rodeo, as cowboys would try to prove their mettle by riding horses that no one else could. Often, wagers would be placed, and cowboys, through the process of amusing themselves on the range, began the sport of rodeo. This sport that evolved from a profession, today, has become a profession of its own.

Top left This photograph was taken at a small rodeo near Colorado Springs in 2000. A roper is superimposed over a wood pattern, creating a stunning visual effect. *Photograph courtesy of Stephen Zacker*

Top right Rodeo has long been staged at the mercy of the elements. This is still true of the many smaller rodeos held throughout the state, like this one in 2003 in Hayden, Colorado, where a girl prepares for her ride. *Photograph courtesy of Matthew Meason*

Above This bull is just relaxing in the hay after a tough day of looking pretty at the 2004 National Western Stock Show. Rodeos are often accompanied by other events relating to livestock. *Photograph by the author*

Colorado, the Birthplace of Rodeo

*R*ODEO IS THE ONLY MAJOR SPORT that developed in the American West, but its roots go much deeper than merely cowboys on the range. Just the word "rodeo" conjures up images of Spanish vaqueros riding the range and roping cattle, and when an ornery cowboy named Milt Hinkle decided to set his event apart from all of the other roundups across the West in the fall of 1913, he went to the Spanish word for "roundup," which was "rodeo." The term "rodeo" continued to gain popularity and eventually stuck.

In Colorado, the birthplace of rodeo, the sport is very popular. There are rodeos all over the state, from the Gunnison Cattlemen's Days, to the Routt County Fair, to the Head Lettuce Days in Buena Vista, Colorado. County fairs may have a rodeo attached, or the rodeo can be a stand-alone event. Either way, Colorado is home to many rodeos, in the summertime especially, but throughout the year as well. Venues, such as the Denver Coliseum, which was built with rodeo in mind, and the Pepsi Center, which can be transformed into a rodeo venue with lots of dirt and sweat on the part of the crew, allow rodeo to be a year-round sport.

Top Men work with horses at the first rodeo in Colorado Springs. This photograph was taken between 1880 and 1900. *Photograph courtesy of Denver Public Library Western History Collection z-2779*

Bottom left A man performs at the Buffalo Bill Wild West Show between 1890 and 1909. Wild West shows were full of excitement for spectators. *Photograph courtesy of Denver Public Library Western History Collection z-2422*

Bottom right Guy Holt performs at the rodeo grounds at Steamboat Springs in 1903. *Photograph courtesy of Denver Public Library Western History Collection x-13685*

Kid Vaughn rides the horse Fox in Steamboat Springs around 1900. *Photograph courtesy of Denver Public Library Western History Collection x-13683*

Today, the rodeo still reflects its strong Spanish origins. For example, since 1995, one of the biggest events at the National Western Stock Show has been the Mexican Rodeo Extravaganza, which features trick roping and mariachi bands. However, the National Western is only a recent nod to the Spanish heritage of rodeo. In 1976, Pueblo began the first international charro competition during the last weekend of August although it is no longer held today. Most of the events at this competition were judged on skill instead of the clock, and almost half of the events were floreando, or rope art, a marked difference from the Americanized rodeo events such as steer wrestling where strength is more important than precision. Another major difference is that the charros hold on to the animals in rough stock events with both hands while in American rodeo, only one hand may be used.

Regardless of the roots of rodeo, the birthplace of the sport of American rodeo is considered to be Deer Trail, Colorado, in 1869. This was an acknowledged fact as early as 1889 when Denver's *Field and Farm Magazine* reported "one of the 'classic' chronicles of an inter-camp cowboy competition were the Bronco Busting contests held on July 4, 1869, at Deer Trail, Colorado." A group of cowboys from neighboring ranches gathered to show off their skills and prowess in an event that would win one of the competitors a

T.N.T. FOR CLYDE HAWKINS.
GOLDEN COLO. RODEO.
ROCKY MT. Photo Co.
DENVER.

A rodeo held in Golden, Colorado, in 1925, featured a horse named TNT, who has just thrown its rider, Clyde Hawkins. *Photograph by Rocky Mountain Photo Company, courtesy of Denver Public Library Western History Collection z-700*

new suit of clothing. Contestants from the Hashknife, Mill Iron, and Campstool Cattle outfits participated in the bronc riding and calf roping events. In some ways, this first rodeo resembled modern rodeos. However, important differences existed.

One of the biggest differences was in the bronc riding competition. Here, there was no stopping after a few seconds. Instead, contestants were forced to ride their mounts until the horses tired. In the case of the winning bronc buster, that translated into fifteen minutes on Montana Blizzard, a fierce horse that gallantly tried to throw its rider. That rider was no Westerner either; he was an English gentleman by the name of Emilnie Gardenshire. This first rodeo had no chutes, no fences, and no stopwatches. One of the ways in which this rodeo did resemble modern rodeos is in how the mounts were assigned. Each ranch had a few "outlaw" horses. These were the horses that couldn't be broken, and each of the contestants at this first rodeo drew lots to see who would ride each animal. According to accounts of this event, "saddles were allowed, but stirrups could not be tied under the horse, and the rider could not use spurs." So these cowboys saddled their outlaw horses and rode them as long as they could. The winner would receive a suit of clothing.

Today, all that is left of that historic meeting of man and outlaw horse is

This old building is located in Deer Trail, Colorado, which would have been a thriving town when the first cowboy contest was held there in 1869. *Photograph by Dino G. Maniatis*

an annual rodeo and a small marker in Deer Trail that reads: "At first, the rodeo had no chutes or fences or deadlines, just a cowboy and a horse, and the open prairie.... [T]hrough the years the rules have changed, but to this day, rodeo remains a match between willful cowboy and unwilling beast." Thus, rodeo was born. According to Ralph Taylor, a Colorado journalist of the 1960s, "It was natural for cowboy tournaments to start in Colorado. Calf ropers came from the plains, and the bronc riders generally were from the mountains where wild horses were to be found."

From its slight beginnings, rodeo began to evolve because of the changing force of civilization that was rapidly taking over the West. Fencing of the range began in the 1880s and led farmers and ranchers to settle down. After settling, they began to hold fairs to exhibit their wares. Afternoons at these gatherings lent themselves to cowboy competitions to show the skills they had picked up on the range. One of the oldest annual rodeos, the Meeker Range Call, was established in 1885 and today is still going strong with four days of celebration scheduled around the Fourth of July with a rodeo, a re-enactment of the Last Ute Indian Uprising, and a 5k run. These contests were still without fences; however, that would change with the Montrose Fair of 1887. Here, an incident convinced cowboys and spectators alike that a proper arena was needed to enjoy the contest safely. Accounts of the event as retold by Ralph Taylor describe the carnage: "The animal made a dash to where the ladies were seated and could not be checked before he struck Mrs. James A. Ladd." After this event and others like it, fences and arenas became the order of the day, leaving only the cowboys to risk life and limb in the arena while the spectators watched from a place of safety, for the most part. There are still times when photographers who get too close to the action are trampled by the animals.

Rodeos were becoming major events for both spectators and for participants. The owner of Commons Park, John Brisben Walker, staged one of the earliest rodeos held in Denver on what is today the site of Union Station. This rodeo, which ostensibly celebrated the Festival of Mountain and Plain, drew a capacity crowd of eight thousand to its events. It also had an elaborate prize list that corresponded to each event. The Class One Winner who had the best time in catching and saddling a wild bronc walked out with fifty dol-

Mayme Stroud is trick riding at the 1921 State Fair in Pueblo, Colorado. Many rodeos feature performers other than cowboys to entertain the crowds between events. *Photograph by Rocky Mountain Photo Company, courtesy of Denver Public Library Western History Collection z-640*

lars, while the Class Six Winner who picked up twenty potatoes the quickest while going at a lope or faster received a silver inlaid bit donated by a publishing house. The bit was worth thirty dollars.

Denver fancied rodeo, and in 1887, the first regularly scheduled rodeo took place in Denver at the Denver Exposition, sponsored by local businesses. It was billed as a cowboy tournament, and thirty cowboys registered. The events included catching, saddling, and riding a wild bronco; roping and hog-tying a wild steer; tailing a steer (roping of a wild steer by two men and stretching him out for branding); foot roping of a cattle from bareback; and, finally, picking up a potato by a rider going faster than a lope. The contestants included many local cowboys. One man, registering as Dull Knife, had the flashiest outfit by far but failed to place in the money. This proved that substance is a more important requirement than style in rodeo, regardless of the time period. This early rodeo caught the attention of the Colorado Humane Society, and the Humane Society immediately began to protest the event on the basis of cruelty toward the animals involved. This was to be the beginning of a long-standing adversarial relationship between rodeo and animal rights groups. The Denver Chamber of Commerce, a major sponsor of the event, responded to the protests by eliminating the tailing event. This did not pacify the Humane Society, but despite the protests, the Denver Exposition showed a profit of four thousand dollars in two days.

The following year, both the Boulder County Industrial Association and the Colorado State Fair in Pueblo held cowboy races. The one at the state fair was five miles long with the riders switching mounts every mile, which made for an exciting show at the mile markers. The state fair had always had Wild West shows ranging from Pawnee to Buffalo Bill. These shows would gradually become cowboy tournaments that would eventually become the rodeo we know today. However, this would be a gradual process that would occur throughout the state in fits and starts. By 1890, a tournament of cowboys was planned for the city of Denver at the Broadway Athletic Park. This rodeo had events ranging from roping and branding to potato racing. This was a highly controversial event; the mayor of Denver at the time, Wolfe Londoner, threatened to arrest everyone if the event was held. The local Humane Society also protested the event because of the innate cruelty to animals that occurs during events such as branding. The show did go on, and this became the first cowboy contest held under electric lights. After all of the problems with this event, Denver backed away from cowboy contests, a tradition that would endure until the National Western Stock Show began its rodeo in 1931.

Bill Baker calf ropes at the Colorado State Fair between 1900 and 1910. *Photograph by Rocky Mountain Photo Company, courtesy of Denver Public Library Western History Collection z-572*

Around the turn of the century, it was often difficult to distinguish between Wild West shows and what would become known as rodeos. Wild West shows were regular visitors to Colorado at this time. One promoter, Arizona Charlie, made his way from Denver to Pueblo to Leadville in 1895, with the Humane Society dogging his steps throughout and actually stopping the show in Denver. Despite its attempts, the Humane Society could not keep the cowboys down. Thad Sowder was a popular and famous cowboy both in Colorado and in Wyoming. His skills were legendary at the time. He won the Denver Horse Show Association bronc riding contest and the title in the Denver Festival of Mountain and Plain. In fact, this man was so famous that he is the mascot of the University of Wyoming and the cowboy seen on all Wyoming license plates. He was the quintessential cowboy, who in the end joined Buffalo Bill's Wild West Show to help bring the American West to the rest of the world.

Another area in which cowboys could demonstrate skill on a horse was beginning to take off in Colorado after the turn of the century. This was the Western movie business. Colorado was home to two motion picture companies during the silent film era, the Selig Polyscope Company and the Colorado Motion Picture Company, both of which were making films featuring men on horseback. Casting cowboys was an obvious choice. Colorado was an important area for the early film industry, and one of the most famous early Westerns was shot here, *The Great Train Robbery*. These Western films

Two men ride toward a crate in Grand Lake, Colorado. This photo was taken sometime between 1900 and 1920. *Photograph courtesy of Denver Public Library Western History Collection x-8735*

A cowboy is thrown from a bucking bronco in Steamboat Springs, Colorado, in 1921. *Photograph by M. E. Helgesen, courtesy of Denver Public Library Western History Collection x-13686*

Opposite

Top A cowboy rides a bronco at the Meeker rodeo between 1890 and 1910. *Photograph courtesy of Denver Public Library Western History Collection x-12449*

Bottom The July 4, 1913, Meeker Range Call parade. This rodeo is one of the oldest in the state, dating back to the late 1800s. *Photograph courtesy of Denver Public Library Western History Collection x-12451*

featured daring stunts to thrill the audience and required able-bodied men who could ride a horse and perform these stunts for the camera. Many cowboys got work this way. This was a job that was somewhere between the Wild West show and the range, as the cowboy actors had to ride and rope with apparent ease, allowing them to show the art of the cowboy to a wider audience. Of course, this was before the perfection of stunts in moviemaking, and many accidents occurred. Horses stomped on actors; actresses fell off horses while in the process of being rescued and were knocked unconscious. In other words, these athletes were injured in the same ways as their rodeo counterparts were, but at least their money was guaranteed. For rodeo cowboys in the arena, there were no guarantees.

Meanwhile, early rodeo continued to develop and evolve, especially in the small towns and communities throughout Colorado. Contests sprung up in Glenwood Springs, at the Montrose Fair, at the Delta County Fair, at the Las Animas County Fair, at the State Fair in Pueblo, and as part of Independence Day celebrations statewide in towns such as Telluride. According to its Web site, Gunnison claims to hold Colorado's oldest annual rodeo, established in 1900. This does not take into account the rodeo first held in 1885 in Meeker, Colorado, but it is an impressive record regardless. While the sport had not yet been christened with the rodeo name, the culture of Colo-

Meeker Colo. July 4th 1913

rado was racing to embrace these contests as more and more small towns and communities rushed to add their own contests for the entertainment of all. Rodeo was quickly becoming a major phenomenon in Colorado, and it was gradually evolving into the rodeo we know today.

This evolution would also include the development of rodeo clowns. The first rodeo clowns were usually injured cowboys whose job was to protect the rough stock riders who were in danger from the animals. They have gradually evolved into a specialized profession of their own, complete with schools and training, and they are crucial for keeping the athletes safe once they have been thrown from their animals. Clowns are one of the more important aspects of rodeo, and they are usually overlooked because of their antics. That clowning around saves lives, and many cowboys who have been thrown from their mounts can attest to the skills of this group of men who risk their own lives by distracting large, angry animals away from defenseless, thrown riders.

The position and prestige of the rodeo clown was not the only thing that was changing. Today, Radical Ryan Rodriquez is a celebrity in his own right who performs during breaks in the action using props such as trampolines and fireworks to keep the crowd from getting restless. A rodeo clown is a combination of stand-up comedian and bull-rider bodyguard. He must be out protecting the cowboys because horses in the arena would just become targets for the bulls.

The contests were also changing as rodeo evolved. The standards of the cowboy contest were not well established or standardized at this time, and there was always room for improvement and innovation. In 1900, that innovation came in the form of a cowboy named Bill Pickett at the Arkansas Valley Fair in Rocky Ford, Colorado. Bill Pickett was a black cowboy, the first to be inducted into the Cowboy Hall of Fame, who took a life-threatening event in the ring and turned it into a brand new event. Ralph Taylor describes the happening in his newspaper column: "The bull tossed Pickett overhead, but the cowboy held onto the horns. In effect it was a fall for the bull.... [H]e grabbed the animal's horns again and twisted his neck until the big bull was compelled to fall. This brought cheer from the crowd." Bulldogging, also known as steer wrestling,

A Sky Chief makes a jump at the 1958 National Western Stock Show with rider Sandy Phipps. *Photography courtesy of Tom Noel Collection*

This photo, taken as a part of the WPA Writers' Program, is of a Will Rogers Rodeo that took place in Manitou Springs between 1930 and 1940. *Photograph courtesy of Denver Public Library Western History Collection x-1677*

was born. This is the event that truly pits man against beast, where man must be strong, fast, and fearless. During the 1960s, Denver Broncos football player John Hatley of Uvalde, Texas, used to bulldog during the off-season, making the size of his fellow players seem not so bad by comparison. When one wrestles a steer weighing upwards of 1,500 pounds, a linebacker of 250 pounds becomes a small nuisance, comparatively speaking.

As Colorado moved further into the twentieth century, more and more rodeos began to establish themselves. Some of these rodeos would become annual events that would attract competitors from all over the country. In 1937, the first Will Rogers Rodeo was held near Colorado Springs in what was known as Will Rogers Stadium. This arena held ten thousand fans and was located across the street from the famous Broadmoor Hotel. Eventually, both the venue and name of this rodeo would change, but it lives on as a successful and popular rodeo today. It has become the Pikes Peak or Bust Rodeo, and now it is one of the top twenty rodeos sanctioned by the Professional Rodeo Cowboys Association (PRCA). This means that the top cowboys from all over the country come to Colorado Springs to compete, to earn points, and to raise their standings. This rodeo once featured horse races, including a wild horse race where contestants had to catch a horse

The 1960 RCA champions are pictured at the 1961 National Western Stock Show on January 19. *Photograph courtesy of Tom Noel Collection*

with two "muggers," or partners who helped to control the horse. The riders would then have to halter and saddle the horse. Next, they would race the beleaguered animal to the far end of the arena and back. Once that was accomplished, the horse had to be unsaddled and the saddle carried across the finish line.

The Pikes Peak or Bust Rodeo is not the only big rodeo with deep roots in Colorado. In 1922, an event known only as Greeley Spud Days got its start. This local celebration featured the Spud Rodeo and Races with livestock provided by local farmers, pies for the pie-eating contest provided by the local ladies of Greeley, and entertainment provided by everyone, from the cowboys to the competitors in the Two-Mile Ford Free-for-All. In this event, Ford automobiles would be driven four laps on a half-mile track. After the first lap, contestants would change a tire; after the second, they would change a spark plug; and after the third lap, they would have to add a quart of oil. From this first Spud Days, an impressive and important rodeo for the state of Colorado would emerge.

By 1925, the livestock used in the rodeo in Greeley was the same used at Cheyenne Frontier Days, and eventually the citizens of Greeley were able to witness the antics of horses such as Midnight and Five Minutes to Midnight, two of the most impressive horses the rodeo world has seen to date. Of course, rodeos would first have to survive the threat of the Woman's Christian Temperance Union (WCTU). In 1928, the WCTU almost managed to cancel the rodeo because of the "noise of the happy celebrants." The women did not approve of the cowboy lifestyle and were willing to protest to end the party even if they were unsuccessful. By 1955, the Spud Rodeo had changed its name to Go West Greeley and was holding chariot races and adding barrel races for the women. By 1971, the name was changed again to the Greeley Independence Stampede, which would remain its name until 2004 when the Rocky Mountain Stampede was born. Regardless of its name, this annual Fourth of July rodeo is still a major stop for those looking to compete in the National Finals Rodeo in Las Vegas.

Sadly, not all rodeos were to be successful during the early twentieth century, and many have come and gone. Some of these rodeos were developed because of the popularity of a neighboring rodeo. The Durango Spanish Trails Fiesta was created in 1919 upon the success of the Ski Hi Stampede, which was founded in Monte Vista that same year. The Spanish Trails Fiesta in Durango, Colorado, was originally held annually starting in 1935, and according to publicity for the rodeo, it "was to be staged not alone for entertainment value, but to retain for its posterity the colorfulness of the

Cy Tallon, pictured at the Monte Vista Ski Hi Stampede, is one of the rodeo announcers in the PRCA Hall of Fame. *Photograph courtesy of Tom Noel Collection*

Clem McSpadder was a president of the PRCA, a United States senator, and a rodeo announcer. *Photograph courtesy of Tom Noel Collection*

Below The family of Governor McNichols at the 1959 National Western Stock Show. The Stock Show has always been a place to see and be seen for both politicians and celebrities. *Photograph courtesy of Tom Noel Collection*

Miss Rodeo Colorado Cassidy Reid carries the Colorado flag during the singing of the National Anthem at the 2004 National Western Stock Show Rodeo. Colorado is a state with a long rodeo tradition. *Photograph by the author*

Opposite This statue of a bronc buster appears in Civic Center Park in Denver, Colorado. Rodeo is a major part of Colorado's heritage. *Photograph courtesy of Tom Noel Collection*

lives and businesses of the pioneers and ranchers of the picturesque San Juan Basin Rodeo Association." During World War II, many rodeos were put on hold, including the Spanish Trails. This event was reborn as an annual event again in 1946, with the Durango High School Band as its official musical accompaniment.

By 1946, it was a Rodeo Cowboys Association–sponsored event, and it was also a great cultural experience for those who attended. Other entertainments at the rodeo included Native American dances and horse races. The first photographed horse race finishes were at the Fiesta. Those who traveled to Durango could also experience some of the natural wonders from Mesa Verde to Aztec National Park, advertised in the official program with the motto "Stay and Play." Advertising tourist attractions was such a good idea that it was copied by the Pikes Peak or Bust Rodeo in Colorado Springs in 1955, which also had a program full of photos of sites ranging from the Garden of the Gods to, ironically enough, Pikes Peak. This rodeo would eventually meet its demise in 1966, as it was "no longer self supporting,"

according to an editorial in the *Durango Herald*. The paper then went on to cite public apathy and the fact that local hotels and shops were no longer interested in the rodeo as additional reasons why the rodeo should not go on. Thus, the Spanish Trails Fiesta ended its run.

In 1923, the Knights of Columbus, a Catholic men's group, held the United States Championship Rodeo. This event met with much difficulty as the Humane Society opposed the cruelty to animals while the Ku Klux Klan opposed the Catholics. This was the period in Denver's history when the Klan ran the show, and many prominent citizens, including Mayor Stapleton, were members of the group. Their opposition ensured that the rodeo was a bust and would never be held again. The Rodeo Cowboys Association would address the problems with the Humane Society in the 1930s. Members would draw up a list of rules to protect the animals involved in the sport of rodeo. The Professional Rodeo Cowboys Association currently has sixty rules and regulations in place for the welfare of the animals. A short list includes the following:

☛ No locked rowels, or rowels that will lock on spurs, may be used on bareback horses or saddle broncs. Spurs must be dulled.

☛ Animals for all events shall be inspected before the draw. No sore, lame, or sick animals, or animals with defective eyesight, shall be permitted in the draw at any time.

☛ A rodeo committee shall ensure that a veterinarian is present for every performance and section of slack.

☛ If a member abuses an animal by any unnecessary, non-competitive or competitive action, he may be disqualified for the remainder of the rodeo and fined $250 for the first offense, with that fine progressively doubling with each offense thereafter. Any member guilty of mistreatment of livestock anywhere on the rodeo grounds shall be fined $250 for the first offense, with that fine progressively doubling with any offense thereafter.

☛ No stock shall be confined or transported in vehicles for a period beyond 24 hours without being properly fed, watered and unloaded.

Despite these rules for the sake of the animals, it would take a few years before a successful rodeo would be held in Denver at the National Western Stock Show, and despite these rules, the rodeo profession is still given a hard time by animal rights groups today. While the Humane Society still protests many rodeos, the most vocal protesters are with an organization known as

PETA, People for the Ethical Treatment of Animals. Today, PETA is working on its "Buck the Rodeo" campaign, claiming on its Web site that the sport of rodeo is "an abusive spectacle that has no place in a civilized society." Rodeo has long been at odds with groups like this, and it doesn't appear that the tensions will ease any time soon.

As for the big city in Colorado—Denver—it remained behind the curve when it came to annual rodeos. With many failed attempts at an annual rodeo, it would take until the 1930s, and a silver anniversary, for the city to actually hold a proper rodeo that would be a success from year to year. In 1931, the National Western Stock Show, which began meeting on an annual basis in 1906 to show and sell animals to other buyers throughout the West, decided to add a rodeo to its festivities in celebration of its twenty-fifth year. The *Denver Post* publicized the event by noting: "With the idea of providing something different for the Silver Jubilee show, the committee has gone to great expense in introducing a rodeo in connection with the horse show."

A comic in the *Denver Post* depicts the addition of the rodeo to the National Western Stock Show in 1931. *Photograph courtesy of Tom Noel Collection*

The Catch-a-Calf competition has long been a Stock Show tradition. This photograph was taken at the 1991 event. *Photograph courtesy of Tom Noel Collection*

The rodeo would be a success due in part to its biggest star, a bucking bronc named Midnight, a champion bucking horse that, according to the January 15 edition of the *Post,* "has thrown some so hard they could not get up." The stage was set for what would become a record-breaking year for the Stock Show and the inaugural year for the "big indoor rodeo," as it was described in an advertisement in an Omaha newspaper.

The Stock Show of 1931 officially opened on January 19, and the horses and their riders played to a crowd of Shriners and high society, with the cowboy's championship bareback riding as the first event of the year. The bareback riding was interspersed with the traditional horse show, which had been the standard fare of the Stock Show in the past. The rodeo experiment was a hit from its inception as described in an article in the January 17 edition of the *Denver Post:*

> While it must not be forgotten that the cultured high hatting dress suit horses from steam-heated stables are to have their inning, all the

broadcasting Saturday was about the untamed brutes from the sticks.
… Lead [*sic*] by the most unmannered crude loud snorting brute named Midnight, this great gang of horse heathens busted through the gates of the stadium.

The rodeo was off to a strong start, and the local newspapers could not gush enough about the wonders of the rodeo. Comments in the press ranged from, "Wild horses and cowboys set Silver Jubilee off with a bang," to "If the first day was a success the second was a WOW! 'Let her Buck' and 'Ride 'em Cowboy' were heard above the applauding thousands," and, finally, this high praise from *Denver Post* writer Edith Eudora Kohl: "If you have seen a thousand rodeos or if you've never seen one, this one will make every drop of red blood run faster."

Cowboys and bucking animals were to replace respectable young women. Well-behaved horses were to be replaced by the meanest, nastiest horses that could be found in the world. No longer would the challenge be to look good on the horse; instead, the challenge would become how long you could stay on the horse. Riding a horse was a life-and-death struggle. Kohl went on to rhapsodize about the contestants: "Cowboys, these world famous riders and ropers … fearlessly take their lives into their hands every time they step foot in the stirrup of the lawless vicious horses they ride."

With its spills and thrills, rodeo is an uncertain sport for those who participate, and the cowboys are not always victorious. Many were rushed to medical facilities for various injuries during the 1931 show. Bob Wright dislocated his hip while attempting to ride a wild Brahma steer; he was rushed to Denver General Hospital, as was twenty-one-year-old Francis Brussear. Owen Crosby, a twenty-two-year-old from Miles City, Montana, was gored by a steer and was operated on at St. Luke's Hospital. Sadly, the most press a losing cowboy could get was if he was seriously injured during the competition. Otherwise, it was the winners and the horses that made headlines at this horse show and rodeo, especially the horse Midnight, who had more press than any of the luckless cowboys who were unfortunate enough to draw this impossible-to-ride horse.

Midnight was the real star of the show. He garnered headlines and photo opportunities that were all but denied to the cowboys who attempted to ride him. During the 1931 rodeo, he was the champ. Of the nineteen men who drew his name for the bronc riding competition, not a single one of them managed to ride this horse, an impressive record for an impressive horse.

Midnight was one of the most fearsome horses of the 1930s. Drawing this bucking bronco usually meant the cowboy would be thrown. *Photograph courtesy of Tom Noel Collection*

Opposite Many rodeos begin with a parade, and the National Western Stock Show's 17th Street Parade is part of that grand tradition. *Photograph courtesy of Tom Noel Collection*

The man who did win the bronc riding competition, Pete Knight, was lucky that he never once drew Midnight.

The birth of the National Western Rodeo coincided nicely with the goals of rodeo cowboys in the 1930s. Rodeo had many fits and starts throughout its history. One of rodeo's goals in the 1930s was to gain respect as a sport. In the early days, rodeo was fairly informal with promoters promising prize money without always delivering. Yet, cowboys as a group were determined to change the system. Their goals were to keep rodeos fair and impartial, to have competent judges at all competitions, and to determine the champion cowboys by a points system based on money earned on the rodeo circuit.

This point system is what made the National Western Stock Show Rodeo so popular from its ciception in 1931. Not only is it the first big rodeo of the year, following the National Finals Rodeo, but also the purse is such that it is worth a cowboy's time to show up and compete. By 1932, the second year of the National Western Stock Show Rodeo, the total prize money was $50,000. By 1982, fifty years later, the prize money was up to $300,000. The National Western Stock Show Rodeo gives cowboys an opportunity to start the year with a bang and big bucks. However, ten years after the first rodeo was held, it would be overshadowed by a much larger conflict, the Second World War. Rodeo experienced many challenges during this period, the first being gas

This youngster takes his first and last steer ride at the 1995 Cattlemen's Days in Gunnison, Colorado. This rodeo claims to be the oldest in the state, having been first held in 1900. *Photograph courtesy of Janet Pharr*

Paul Lang, a bull rider, tries to make eight seconds at a Labor Day Weekend Rodeo in Trinidad in 2000. *Photograph courtesy of Emily Dickinson*

Below Rodeo developed from life on the trail. Cowboys who were without other forms of entertainment would place wagers on who was the best; thus, a sport was born of a profession. In 2003, this group of cowboys in Pagosa, Colorado, carries on that proud tradition. *Photograph courtesy of Karen Godbold*

A steer wrestler works to subdue an animal that weighs five times what he does. This event is one of the later additions to rodeo, having been developed by Bill Pickett in 1900. *Photograph courtesy of R. Woolmington*

Below Dad is the header while his son is the heeler in the team roping event at the Yuma County Fair of August 2003. Rodeo is a family event. *Photograph courtesy of Pat Armagost*

Above J. C. Trujillo on Satin and Velvet in 1998. *Photograph by Jim Fain, courtesy of Tom Noel Collection*

Right The hardest part of a wild horse race is getting a rider on the uncooperative horse. This team struggles to complete that task in Grover, Colorado, in 2003. *Photograph courtesy of Tanya Wahlert*

This man has finally managed to get on his mount in the wild horse race at the Earl Anderson Memorial Rodeo in Grover, Colorado, in June of 2003. *Photograph courtesy of Tanya Wahlert*

Below In the struggle between man and beast, man is often the loser. Many cowboys spend a lot of time eating dust. *Photograph courtesy of Tim Rudnick*

Top left This is an old rodeo arena located in Burns, Colorado. While time may have ravaged this particular venue, the sport continues on into the twenty-first century. *Photograph courtesy of Jocelyn Mauch*

Right Clint Lay works to rope his calf at the 2003 Elbert County Fair. This is a skill that would have been used on a cattle drive in the late 1800s. Today, it is a skill rodeo cowboys perform to entertain crowds. *Photograph courtesy of Suni Olkjer*

Center left Bull riding is the most dangerous part of rodeo. A rider must remain on the bull for eight seconds to receive a score. The score is based on the performances of both the cowboy and the bull. *Photograph courtesy of Reesa Isbell*

Bottom These two men work together to subdue a steer in the team roping event. This is one of the five main events at any rodeo and has been since almost the beginning of the sport. *Photograph courtesy of Tim Rudnick*

Above This lone cowboy makes the art of twirling a rope seem almost effortless as he and his horse work together to rope a calf. *Photograph courtesy of Charlie Powell*

Below Wearing a pair of very fashionable chaps, this bareback rider attempts to complete his ride at the 2003 Elizabeth Stampede. Chaps were originally worn to protect the legs of a rider on the open range. Today, they can be quite the fashion statement. *Photograph courtesy of Jodie Mooney*

Above A well-trained horse is key in calf roping. The horse must keep the rope taut while the cowboy runs to finish tying up the calf as quickly as possible. If the horse doesn't do its job, the calf becomes more difficult to control. *Photograph courtesy of Reesa Isbell*

Right A bareback rider loses his seat in Sterling, Colorado. The first rodeos had no time limits. A cowboy would ride a bucking horse until either the cowboy or the horse was exhausted. *Photograph courtesy of Reesa Isbell*

Below These horses at the Larimer County Fair Grounds in Loveland, Colorado, are resting before the excitement begins at the rodeo in 2003. The cowboys behind them are also getting ready for their moments in the ring. *Photograph courtesy of Suni Olkjer*

rationing and its effects on travel. The government allowed sporting events to take place during the war, but getting from point to point caused problems. This forced cowboys to save gas coupons and to carpool to events scattered throughout the country. Another problem facing the cowboys who stayed home was the perception that they were able-bodied men who should have been fighting for their country. In reality, many cowboys did go to war. In fact, Fritz Truan, the world champion saddle bronc rider of 1939, died in service to his country at Iwo Jima.

Yet, Uncle Sam was reluctant to take all comers. Many of the cowboys who remained at home were disabled in ways that prevented them from serving their country in an obvious fashion, and the government didn't want to gamble with old rodeo injuries flaring up while these cowboys were on duty. Instead, they stayed on the home front and kept up the spirits of Americans during the war. They simply did what they did best, rodeo, while their organizations were busy pushing the sale of war bonds to show the patriotism of rodeo cowboys. Cowboys were also looking at changes in the sport. The 1940s saw the end of two hands being used in rough stock events. For bareback riding, a suitcase rigging would be developed so that cowboys could hang on a bit better than by clutching the horse's mane.

A program from the 1998 National Western Stock Show displays the lights of the city and county building in the background. The lights are kept on until the Stock Show leaves town. *Photograph courtesy of Tom Noel Collection*

In the era following World War II, rodeos in Colorado began to boom. Colleges and high schools began to form teams, and many counties and towns throughout the state started their own rodeos and horse shows. One example is the Arapahoe County Fair, which was first held in 1947. This event featured typical rodeo contests such as bronc riding and steer wrestling. It also featured a series of free-for-all races with a chariot race. Today, the Arapahoe County Fair is an annual event held in Deer Trail, Colorado, the site of the first rodeo in the world. Rodeo has come full circle, and today it is a link to a past that is quickly disappearing in the modern world.

CHAPTER 2

The Business of Rodeo

*D*URING THE NINETEENTH CENTURY, as America expanded its boundaries and its people farther and farther west, they brought with them many different types of livestock. Oxen, horses, mules, and cows were driven onto the prairies of modern-day Kansas and Colorado. This pushed the native tribes and the buffaloes out as the cow gained a foothold in an environment that was almost ideally suited to its well-being. Soon, the cattle industry was born. As any successful cattleman knows, with cattle comes responsibility. Someone must keep a lookout over the valuable product and ensure its safety. Thus, the cowboy was born. A typical day on the range had cowboys roping cattle, branding cattle, and herding cattle. Today, we as Americans have moved further and further from our agricultural roots, and cowboys have redirected their energies from the range to the modern rodeo. Rodeo is also a big business that has gone through many fits and starts as it worked its way from small-time wagers to a multimillion-dollar industry.

After the Civil War, the American West was bursting with cattle. Entrepreneurs began to herd the cattle and drive them to markets where they would be well compensated. However, manpower was needed to get the cattle from

Rodeo began as a profession before it evolved into a sport. Cowboys needed to brand all new calves to prevent them from being stolen or confused with the cattle from another herd. Today, rodeos have become a big business of their own. *Photograph courtesy of Carol Chesney*

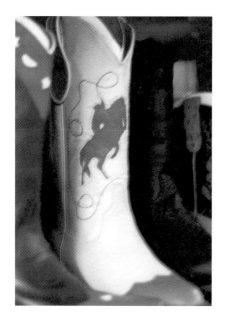

Rodeo is a sport that has its own unique equipment, and these boots definitely reflect the color of the rodeo lifestyle. *Photograph by the author*

the range to the railroads, and many entrepreneurs took a leaf from the book of our neighbors to the south. From the vaqueros, the ideas and practices of the cowboys were developed and perfected. These men lived on the range, tending to their herds. They often found themselves with time on their hands. These bored cowboys began to make friendly wagers on their skills against their colleagues on the range. Who could rope a cow the fastest; who could ride an unrideable horse the longest? Eventually these contests became a spectator sport for those of the West, and by the late 1890s, many towns were holding cowboy contests in an attempt to outdo one another.

One of the best examples of this would be the rivalry that sprung up between Denver and Cheyenne over who should be the real host of the famous Frontier Days, which was first held in 1897 in Wyoming. This rivalry was mentioned in the August 20, 1912, *Wyoming Tribune,* noting that "now comes the annual suggestion from residents of the larger city that, inasmuch as Frontier Days is so successful, the celebration should be appropriated by Cheyenne's big neighbor, Denver, and there made a fete of greater magnitude." Denver had made a few unsuccessful attempts to steal the show, but it had failed. Instead, it would have to console itself with a few sporadic rodeos and Wild West shows to drive its local economy and to help the city to remember its rural heritage, which was quickly fading into the not-so-distant past.

By the 1910s, rodeo had established itself as an important part of the culture of the West, but it had many fits and starts throughout its history. One of the first goals of rodeo was to gain respect as a sport outside the traditional rodeo community. In the early days, rodeo was fairly informal with promoters promising prize money without always delivering. This was a problem for the cowboys, who had to pay transportation expenses and contest entry fees; if the prize money was not delivered, they were often stuck with no reward to show for their travel, time, and skill. Quite often, public sympathy was not with the cowboys, who had earned quite a reputation. Cowboys were notorious for not showing up for events and for getting drunk and causing trouble in the various towns hosting rodeos, which did not endear them to the locals.

In the 1920s, cowboys were competing just as hard as they had around the turn of the century; yet, they were not the most organized group. As the end of the Roaring Twenties neared, many cowboys throughout the country began to push for the formation of a cohesive group, a slow and arduous task. One of the first groups to form was the Rodeo Association of America (RAA), founded in 1929, which worked to standardize rules and the procedure of

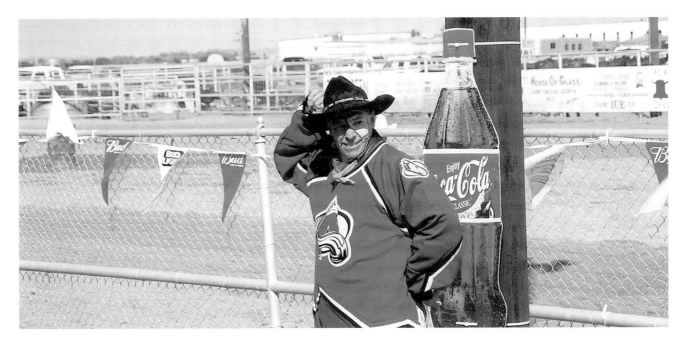

Sponsorship is an important aspect of rodeo. Bobby Weir, a rodeo clown, stands in front of advertisements for cola and beer at the Trinidad Roundup in 2000. *Photograph courtesy of Bernadette Dickinson*

Below The Chuteout Bar at the National Western Stock Show, named after the prestigious Coors Chuteout Rodeo Series, features a neon bar sign with a bull riding cowboy. Notice the belt buckle beer tap in the lower left hand corner complete with cowboy hat. *Photograph by the author*

Rodeo clowns pose for the camera in front of their barrel provided by Coors. Leon Coffee is the man on the far right. He is one of the most famous rodeo clowns of the twentieth century. *Photograph courtesy of Tom Noel Collection*

choosing a champion. The RAA was met with lots of resistance by those whom it was attempting to help—the cowboys. It did achieve some of its goals, such as standardizing a point system to determine rank, based on one and one-half point for every dollar earned for riding events while timed events earned only one point per dollar. The RAA found it difficult to keep track of the money earned by cowboys throughout the country; in 1934, it is believed that the all-around champion never once left California to compete in a rodeo, making it a stretch to call him a world champion.

Problems still persisted for the working cowboy, especially when it came to money, but it was the money that was to be the key in the development of the profession of rodeo. In some cases, the purse was smaller than the total of the entry fees of the contestants, which was a definite sore point for the riders who felt that the entry fees should be added to the purse as a matter of principle. Cowboys were also angry about the system used to judge an event. Oftentimes, the judges showed a tendency to give their good acquaintances a better score than the unknown cowboys who were competing in the same events. Many complaints were heard from cowboys throughout the country over this issue. Another criticism directed at the judges was their ignorance of the events they were judging. They may have been impartial, but they did not understand the subtleties of the sport, which made it difficult for them to give an accurate score. Changes were desperately needed if rodeo was going to become a respectable sport.

By 1936, the cowboys who were being taken advantage of had hit their limits. They demanded that the purses be doubled at the Boston Rodeo in Massachusetts by augmenting the original purse prize with the entry fees paid by every contestant. As the purse stood, not even the overall winners would have made traveling expenses at this rodeo. The cowboys threatened a strike and had even procured their tickets home ahead of time to prove that they were serious in their demands. If they did not get what they wanted, they would simply leave town. When the show opened, the cowboys refused to ride despite the threats of the promoter to throw their horses into the river. The cowboys responded to these threats by moving their animals to another stable. These events led rodeo cowboys everywhere to stop working, and, in a show of solidarity, the cowboys refused as a group to fill in as scabs. The audience at the Boston Garden was treated to a display of mediocrity. This was unacceptable to the spectators. The promoters were then forced to raise the purses to a reasonable level, and the real cowboys agreed to compete.

The rodeo riders learned from this experience; they learned that if they stuck together, they could accomplish things instead of remaining at the mercy of the rodeo promoters. This was quite a shift from the solitary loner on the range, who is self-sufficient and dependent upon no one, or as anthropologist Elizabeth Atwood put it, "the archetypal lone cowboy." The idea of the cowboy union was beginning to be accepted by the cowboys in an era when unionization was popular—the Great Depression. This group was known as the Cowboys Turtle Association (CTA), or the Turtles for short. There are a couple of different explanations for this odd name. One version states that the turtleneck sweaters worn by the group was the reason behind the clever moniker. Others claim that the name reflected the slow movement of the group, especially at the beginning of the process, which was similar to the slow movement of turtles. In the end, they finally stuck their necks out to

Above Brad Tilton attempts to ride a bucking bronc at the 2002 Rimrock Rodeo in Fruita, Colorado. The excitement of a rodeo can boost the economy of a small town immensely. *Photograph courtesy of Cindy Ferguson*

Right This horse appears to be kind and gentle, but only if you stay off him. He was one of the bucking broncs at the High Country Stampede Rodeo in August 2003. *Photograph courtesy of Debbie Wolf*

Far right Livestock contractors are an important part of rodeo. Many have made it into the Pro Rodeo Hall of Fame. Stock contractors provide the bulls and bucking broncs for the rough stock events. *Photograph courtesy of Becky Pagnotta*

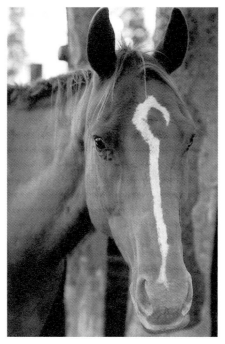

accomplish something together. Despite the confusion over the name's origin, the goals of this group were very simple: to keep rodeos fair and impartial and to have competent judges at all competitions. Thankfully, the scoring system for rodeo developed by the RAA was already in place. This would be one less thing for the Turtles to worry about.

Gaining membership into the Turtles was fairly straightforward: for a five-dollar fee, you were a member. The group's rules were published in the December 1936 edition of *Hoofs and Horns* magazine. It required that cowboys and cowgirls caught competing in a rodeo in which a strike had been called would have to pay five hundred dollars; otherwise, they would be blacklisted and prevented from participating in CTA-sanctioned rodeos. That money would then be placed in a trust where it would be used by the Turtles for further strike efforts as needed. Strikes had to be called by all members of the association. Fines could be collected for disgraceful conduct. The Turtles refused to mediate conflicts that occurred between cowboys, but the group did reserve the right to call for new judges during a competition as needed.

Sponsorship is a major part of any rodeo. Here, a horse displays an advertisement for Justin Boots at the 2004 National Western Stock Show. *Photograph by the author*

By 1937, new concerns had arisen. This was reflected in the rules that were passed by the CTA in its second year. The new rules stated that all entry fees had to be added to the purse of a rodeo and that a prize list must be circulated thirty days before the event began. Rodeo judging panels must have two active cowboy contestants, and cowboys who made four rodeos in a year were no longer considered amateurs and must register with the CTA. The designation of amateur versus professional also raged throughout the rodeo world in the 1940s with many disagreements over the status of cowboys as professionals. The issue was eventually resolved in 1957 with the invention of the permit system. This allowed nonmembers to compete in sanctioned rodeos and has become an important tool in developing the young cowboys of today into the world champions of tomorrow.

Lastly added to the new rules, the CTA would pay any bill left by a member; however, that member would become blacklisted if he failed to repay the debt. This last rule was passed to try to change the reckless image of the rodeo cowboy into something respectable. This would be a slow process hindered by the CTA itself. The July 9, 1939, *Saturday Evening Post* published "No Turtles Need Apply," which detailed the struggles of the Turtles to achieve their goals with rodeo promoters at the Pendleton Roundup, which fed into the public's stereotype of the reckless cowboy.

In 1945, the Cowboys Turtle Association would become the Rodeo Cowboys Association (RCA). Rodeo groups were becoming more organized and cohesive. The biggest challenge facing this group in the first years of its existence was the question of how to determine the world champions of each event and the best cowboy overall. At first, points as calculated by a system developed by the RAA determined the victors. This was problematic, as many rodeos did not report money earned to the association. Also, cowboys could accumulate large amounts of points in the larger rodeos, which gave them an unfair advantage over cowboys who only competed in the smaller rodeos. A true world championship rodeo was needed, and the process of planning and setting up such an event began in 1958 at the annual RCA meeting in Denver under the direction of Lex Connoly, who was the only full-time member of the RCA Board. During his tenure, he was responsible for providing insurance for cowboys, promoting national television coverage, and, most importantly, developing the World Champion Rodeo. This was a task that involved cowboys, promoters, sponsors, and stock contractors. The first National Finals Rodeo premiered in 1959 in Dallas, Texas. It was later moved to Los Angeles in 1962, to Oklahoma City by 1965, and today is the culminating event in the rodeo season, held annually in Las Vegas since 1985.

As the sport of rodeo moved into the second half of the twentieth century, it became much more organized. It made its headquarters in Denver, Colorado, in offices located near 17th and Champa Streets. Along with this move into stability came an insurance policy for rodeo cowboys who were injured during the course of competition. The RCA managed to find an insurance company that was willing to cover its cowboys—the Republic National Insurance Company of Dallas, Texas. This company agreed to do this in exchange for either a portion of the membership dues or the money paid for claims, depending upon which amount was larger. Today, HealthSouth, a group that donates its health services to injured cowboys, insures the cowboys on the Professional Bull Riders (PBR) circuit while Justin Sports Medicine looks after the cowboys of the rival PRCA. After all, if any group needed health insurance, it would have to be those who compete against animals weighing ten times what they do.

Many bull riders and bronc riders have begun to wear protective vests. These vests are designed to protect internal organs and help keep a cowboy safer so he can earn more money. This photograph was taken at the Red Ryder Roundup in Pagosa Springs in 2003. *Photograph courtesy of Susan Ammons*

The rates of injury are not helped by the fact that the animals used in rodeo are being bred bigger and stronger. Stock contractors have been trying to create the ultimate in bucking stock for as long as it has been profitable. With today's advances in DNA technology, breeders are able to isolate the traits they want to increase in animals, making them more and more difficult to ride, or as the cowboys put it, "rank." One of the biggest and most famous of the stock contractors is a man named Mike Cervi. Cervi began his career as a rodeo clown, and today, he owns two of the largest stock contracting companies in the world: the Beutler Brothers and Cervi Rodeo Company and Cervi Championship Rodeo Company.

Two brothers named Jake and Lynn Beutler originally ran the Beutler Brothers Company out of Elk City, Oklahoma; Cervi purchased it in 1967. Cervi then went on in 1975 to buy the Billy Minick Rodeo Company, which was once owned by Gene Autry, renaming both companies after himself. Today, Cervi's Circle I brand is one of the most prestigious in rodeo. It is also the second oldest brand in the state, with the motto, "Do or Die for the

A bull rider takes his victory lap after winning day money at the 2004 National Western Stock Show Rodeo. A rodeo queen carrying the flag of the event sponsor, Coors, precedes him. *Photograph by the author*

Circle I." According to his Web site, Cervi has a simple goal for his businesses: "To produce a fast and exciting rodeo with the best bucking stock available." Cervi has met this goal on numerous occasions. In 1983 and 2001, the Professional Rodeo Cowboys Association recognized Cervi as stock contractor of the year. He was also inducted into the Pro Rodeo Hall of Fame as a stock contractor in 2003.

Today's best cowboys can earn millions of dollars competing against livestock that continues to improve. While competing in the arena is the traditional way that cowboys earn their money, the successful modern cowboy also has a few endorsements up his sleeve (and on his sleeve). The same could be said about the traditional rodeo, where advertising and sponsorships are as important as the rodeo action. Half a century ago, the Rodeo Cowboys Association tried to ban product placements by both rodeos and cowboys. Today, ads dominate arenas, and cowboys have their names on everything from beer to colognes. Charmayne James, a world champion barrel racer, has her own brand of ladies cologne. Other big sponsors of rodeos include American truck companies, tobacco companies, and rodeo equipment companies.

Beer and trucks are obvious rodeo sponsors. After all, who can imagine a cowboy driving a BMW and sipping from a bottle of Evian? Cowboys typically drive trucks because they live a lifestyle that requires a truck to haul gear from place to place, and they often enjoy drinking a beer—an American beer. Coors is one of the major sponsors of the Professional Rodeo Cowboys Association; it was the first with a multimillion-dollar contract with the PRCA, and today, it has what is known as the first right of refusal. It gets first shot at sponsorship of the top rodeos the rodeo world has to offer (i.e., the PRCA-sanctioned events). If Coors refuses, the PRCA can then begin talking to other beer sponsors. Coors is also the sponsor of "The Man in the Can" program, which was started in 1983. This is a clever marketing strategy that features bull fighters, better known as rodeo clowns, throughout the country. Forty-five barrel men compete each year for the top spot at the National Finals Rodeo where the winner receives a bronze belt buckle plus ten thousand dollars cash. They are also honored at the Cowboy Hall of Fame in Colorado Springs. Additionally, these men are compensated each time they roll out their Coors barrel to protect the riders.

Sponsorships aside, the real action is in the arena, and in the case of cowboys, points are money—literally. To qualify for the National Finals Rodeo—the goal of any cowboy worth his salt—a cowboy has to be in the top fifteen in his event. This makes the largest rodeos the most desirable because they

This barrel man is using a Coors Original barrel. Barrels provide safety for the humans and advertising for the beer company, which pays a stipend every time its barrel is used. *Photograph courtesy of Deb Ropken*

have the biggest prizes. The *Denver Post* reported in 2004 that a few years ago, cowboys would have to compete in one hundred rodeos. Today, if a cowboy makes it to the big rodeos, it cuts that number down to sixty. Consequently, bigger rodeos attract a lot of cowboys competing for those cash prizes. That is why Denver's National Western Rodeo, with its $520,000 in prize money in 2004, is such an important event and has grown so big that "slack competitions" must be used. This first occurred in 1979 and has been a tradition ever since. A slack event is one of a set of preliminary events without cash prizes that determine who gets to compete for the money in front of an audience. Results are based on the average of competitors' times or scores at the slack events.

Over the last century, the audience has changed as well as the cowboys. The first rodeos took place during the day in the great outdoors. Those who were watching tended to be locals from nearby towns and ranches. From these humble beginnings, rodeo began to move indoors under the lights and to appeal to a larger audience who would have traveled from farther away than the next town over. Today, rodeo has gone high-tech and can be found playing on cable television at all hours of the day. Television coverage of the finals rodeo at the National Western Stock Show first occurred in 1954. It was broadcast on KBTV Channel 9 at 8 p.m. By 1974, CBS paid seven thousand dollars to televise the event, which caused quite a controversy. CBS wanted to make sure that the televised rodeo featured the cream of the crop of champion cowboys, and the Rodeo Cowboys Association agreed. However, many of the champions had already gone home and would have to make a return trip. To entice the cowboys to return and compete for the cameras, National Western officials had to add two thousand dollars to the pot while the RCA added five hundred dollars.

While, on occasion, rodeo promoters have been somewhat reluctant to transition to television, in the digital age, rodeo has been thriving on the airwaves. Today, the rodeo aficionado can get his fix on cable channels such as ESPN and Outdoor Life Network, which have opened up the sport to a much wider and more diverse audience. Traditional rodeo is not the only thing on the tube. The average channel surfer will find that today the bull riders are getting a lot of TV time, especially since there are two competing tours of bull riders. In fact, a rivalry of sorts has developed between the PRCA, which has its featured Xtreme Bulls Tour along with the traditional array of rodeo events, and the Professional Bull Riders, who only ride bulls. The PBR, formed in 1992 after a split from the PRCA, has many televised contests. This has translated into more expensive tickets for live events that sell

Sometimes, the animals get more respect than the cowboys. Here, the bull Little Yellow Jacket is alone in the spotlight at the Professional Bull Riders event at Colorado Springs, Colorado, in 2003. *Photograph courtesy of Sandra Kelch*

out regularly. Meanwhile, the PRCA is fighting back with its Xtreme Bulls Tour. Bull riding has become one of the most popular aspects of rodeo as it is often viewed as an extreme sport by Generation X, and it is leading the charge in attracting a younger demographic to rodeo. A younger demographic translates into higher advertising revenues, and it also allows for rodeo culture to be passed on to people who may have never ridden a horse before, let alone a bull.

This surge in rodeo popularity has been good for many businesses that directly relate to the sport. One of these is the Lancaster Rock-N-Roll Rodeo School, established in 1971 in Arvada, Colorado. The school offers classes in both bull riding and bull fighting for the greenhorn who wants to experience firsthand the adrenaline rush. Lancaster is also very involved in the rodeo equipment business for both bull riding and other rodeo events. Featured products include chaps, priced starting at three hundred dollars, to which the cowboy can add extras such as extra-long fringe or words at five dollars per letter. Protective vests are also available. Helmets and face masks, which are very slowly becoming more popular with bull riders who wish to avoid concussions, are sold as well. These are required gear for anyone wishing to ride a bull at the school.

This bull fighter knows the value of good endorsements. He has Play It Again Sports, Justin Boots, and other sponsors' badges displayed on his shorts. *Photograph courtesy of S. Diamond*

Helmets aside, no cowboy is complete without a proper hat, and some of the best hats in the country come from the southwest corner of Colorado where the O'Farrell Hat Makers of Durango is located. The hats created are not inexpensive, but they are well worth the price, especially when one considers the incredible quality of these world-famous hats. Consumers may choose custom-made hats, which are fitted to an individual's unique head shape using a conformature to precisely map the shape of the head. Customers may also opt for a prefabricated hat in a standard size. In its May 2001 issue, *Forbes* magazine proclaimed these hats as "America's Finest Hats."

Another important piece of equipment for a cowboy or a cowgirl is a saddle. There are different types of saddles for different events. Saddle bronc riders must have what is known as an Association Saddle, which, according to the PRCA, is "a saddle used in bronc riding built to definite PRCA specifications." In other words, it has been approved by the Professional Rodeo Cowboys Association for this event, as has all of the rest of the equipment used, down to the type of fleece protecting the horse. These saddles have been standardized in the twentieth century so that no rider has an advantage over another, which used to be a bit of a problem with some of the older

saddles that would vary from cowboy to cowboy. Today, these saddles usually lack a pommel while roping event saddles tend to have a rubberized pommel, which allows a contestant to easily tie the rope to his horse which is trained to keep the line taut while the cowboy quickly finishes his task.

Some of the best saddle-making companies are located in Colorado. One of these is the Colorado Saddlery Company located in lower downtown Denver. This company was founded in 1940 and makes its saddles the old-fashioned way with no synthetic materials. These saddles are of exceedingly high quality and have developed a loyal following. John Wayne, the Western film star, purchased his saddles through the Colorado Saddlery Company as does Paul Hogan and many other celebrities. Another famous saddle company is the Old Pueblo Saddle Company located in Pueblo, Colorado. This company won a best saddle award at the Colorado State Fair in 1997 and has made saddles for athletes such as basketball player Kareem Abdul-Jabbar. They, too, make their saddles the way they were made in the Old West—with no manmade materials. In fact, saddle maker Allan Byrne is constantly researching the techniques that were used in the Old West to create more authentic saddles. Both of these companies also produce other types of equipment, but it is their saddles that get most of the attention.

As saddles differ, so do horses. These valuable, well-trained animals are an important part of a rodeo team. A barrel-racing horse must be able to run the course quickly yet be controlled enough to not knock over the barrels. This horse must also be able to travel in a horse trailer all over the country. These animals have been known to cost fifty thousand dollars, which constitutes a definite investment in one's event. Those who wrestle steer for a living need a hazer, the guy who attempts to guide the steer on a rather fearless horse while the wrestler himself must be on a fast horse that doesn't mind his rider leaping off of him in the middle of a run. These horses must be in good health to compete in these events, and the care of a horse can be a costly, time-consuming endeavor. Moreover, these horses are an important part of a rodeo contestant's livelihood. In fact, they are just like part of the family in some cases. In all, rodeo is a big and complex business that encompasses the equipment, the stock, and the prize money. It seems almost logical that a sport that evolved from a profession would today have such an elaborate economic influence on the world around it.

Top The Professional Bull Riders tour has many sponsors, including the Ford Motor Company who presents a one thousand dollar check to a winning bull rider at a Professional Bull Riders event in Colorado Springs. *Photograph courtesy of Sandra Kelch*

Bottom While a bull rider fights to stay on his animal, this photograph, taken at a PBR event in Colorado Springs in 2003, highlights the many sponsors that support rodeo and keep the lifestyle alive. *Photograph courtesy of Sandra Kelch*

Rodeo for the Young'uns

RODEO IS A FAMILY AFFAIR; one only has to look at the numerous families that travel around the country going from one rodeo to the next. In order to pass on the traditions to the next generation, rodeo families have to get their children involved early because the only way for young children, or anyone for that matter, to develop the skills needed in rodeo is to teach them at an early age, and then practice, practice, practice. This is true of all sports. There are little league baseball teams, soccer teams for three-year-olds, and pee-wee football teams, and all of these groups are dedicated to developing young athletes, training them, and helping them become the stars of tomorrow in their sport of choice. Rodeo has similar programs to get young boys and girls ready for the pros. These programs allow cowboys of all ages to perfect their skills and to win prizes so they can move on to the next level where they will continue to work on developing as champions. Four-year-olds can go from mutton busters, where they will get their first opportunity to experience the thrill of the sport, to steer riding and to bull riding within a short period of time, allowing for the culture of rodeo to be passed on to the next generation. Those involved in the timed events also

Ross Wahlert, age nine, waits for the calf riding competition to start at the eightieth Grover Rodeo in Grover, Colorado, in 2003. All bull fighters have to start somewhere. *Photograph courtesy of Tanya Wahlert*

Mutton busting is one of the first rough riding events young cowboys and cowgirls experience. This buster hangs on for dear life at the Rim Rock Rodeo in Fruita, Colorado, in 2003. *Photograph courtesy of Judy Morehouse*

go through a progression of events starting with goat tying and advancing into steer roping and team roping.

One of the earliest events open to beginning cowboys and cowgirls is mutton busting. This event is a favorite at many rodeos; it is only open to the young, and usually there is a maximum weight for the little competitors. Contestants are placed on a sheep, generally protected by a padded vest and a hockey-like mask and helmet similar to those just starting to be worn by bull riders. The young mutton buster is then asked to hold on for dear life as the sheep makes a run for the other end of the arena trying to buck off its young rider. The winner is the one that holds on the longest. Some of these young roughriders are so good that they have to be forcibly pried off their sheep at the other end of the arena. This is only the first of the many levels of competition open to the children of rodeo; eventually, if these children stick with the sport, they will participate in the same events as their rodeo heroes, perhaps at places like the National Finals Rodeo.

To that end, many different rodeos have been developed for the younger generations of cowboys and cowgirls. Here in Colorado, there are many rodeo choices for kids who compete; the most famous is the Little Britches

Arabian horses on display at the 1952 National Western Stock Show. This is an event that offers more than just rodeo in the way of equestrian entertainment. *Photograph courtesy of Tom Noel Collection*

Rodeo. This event was first held in Littleton, Colorado, at the Arapahoe County Fair Grounds in 1952 before it went on to become a nationwide phenomenon. By 1958, this rodeo had become the largest amateur junior rodeo in the nation. It boasted 676 competitors, with 283 competing in senior boys Brahma bull riding and 296 in senior boys bareback riding.

The ages of the competitors ranged from eight to eighteen, and these athletes came from all over North America from cities as far away as New Iberia, Louisiana, and Alberta, Canada. Events included the standard rodeo fare as well as some more unusual events such as wild cow milking. Here, five young men worked together "to tangle with a vicious, plunging, kicking, rearing, wild cow," as described in the Little Britches program. Four members of the team worked to control the cow while the fifth attempted to milk the cow into a soda pop bottle.

This rodeo would become the training ground for young cowboys who would someday become world champions. After all, the Little Britches slogan is "Where legends begin." Men such as Ty Murray, the King of the Cowboys, got their start in the Little Britches Rodeo. For Murray, it was the beginning of an illustrious and legendary career in the sport, as he retired in 2002 with

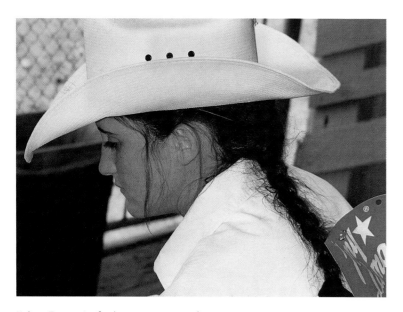

Kelsey Tate waits for her next event at the Little Britches Rodeo in Rifle, Colorado, in 1999. Little Britches is one of the largest youth rodeo groups in the United States. *Photograph courtesy of Marlene Tate*

lifetime earnings of more than $3 million, having been named all-around cowboy champion seven times and awarded many other honors, prizes, and titles throughout his fourteen-year career.

The rodeo continued at the Arapahoe County Fair Grounds for a number of years until 1961 when the Little Britches organization held a national convention in Denver. It was decided that the Little Britches would go national and Denver would be its headquarters. Eventually, this rodeo, named after a book of the same name written by local author Ralph Moody, would outgrow its Denver location and move to its present headquarters in Colorado Springs in 1982. Today, this is where its finals rodeo is held every year. Participants from around the country gather to prove once and for all who the best cowboys and cowgirls are. Currently, this "little" rodeo association holds rodeos in thirty different states, with over seventeen hundred young athletes participating in the program. This popular rodeo has been covered by local television stations and has been filmed by Walt Disney film crews. In short, it is one of the premier youth rodeos in the country.

However, the Little Britches of Colorado was the first and "the grandbaby of them all," established to provide youngsters with their very own rodeo. The Little Britches program is not just designed to create rodeo stars; good sportsmanship is also an important area of emphasis for these young cowboys and cowgirls. According to its mission statement, the Little Britches is "a nonprofit venture to build sound, healthy minds and bodies—to develop character, self-reliance and good sportsmanship through competition in the great sport of rodeo."

This rodeo is divided by age category. The youngest participants range in age from five to seven years old; this coed group is known as the Little Wranglers. These children compete in four events: barrel racing, pole bending, flag racing, and goat tail untying. The next age group is divided by gender into the Junior Girls and Junior Boys. Their ages range from eight to thirteen years old. The girls' events at this level are breakaway roping, barrel racing, goat tying, trail course, and pole bending. The boys compete in bareback riding, steer riding, bull riding, breakaway roping, goat tying, and

This young cowboy gets some advice from a more seasoned cowboy, passing the culture of rodeo from one generation to the next. *Photograph courtesy of the Schowalter family*

Below left Kelsey Tate, age thirteen, is pictured at a 1999 Little Britches Rodeo event in Rifle, Colorado, having won a seventh place ribbon. *Photograph courtesy of Marlene Tate*

Below Not everyone is cut out for rodeo. This young girl is not a happy camper at the Saddle Saloon at Pueblo in 2000. *Photograph courtesy of Becky Pagnotta*

The cowboy on the right wears a Colorado State High School Rodeo Association Finals jacket. Just like the pros, high school athletes have a championship rodeo. *Photograph courtesy of Stephanie Seifried*

flag racing. One coed event exists at this level, dally ribbon roping, which is also known as team roping. The oldest groups are the Senior Girls and Senior Boys, and they compete from age fourteen until age eighteen. Boys compete in steer wrestling, saddle bronc riding, bareback riding, bull riding, and tie-down roping while girls compete in breakaway roping, barrel racing, goat tying, trail course, and pole bending. The boys and girls compete together in the team roping competition. These young contestants must adhere to strict guidelines. Participants can be disqualified for abuse of stock, officials, or other contestants. Also, the winners are never awarded money, as the Little Britches is an amateur competition. Instead, winners receive various prizes ranging from saddles and belt buckles to college scholarships.

Today, the National Little Britches Finals Rodeo is held in Penrose Stadium in Colorado Springs, Colorado. This event is estimated to bring $8.5 million into the Springs as six hundred youngsters compete to see who is the best of the best and who will win the $30,000 in scholarship money. To get to this point, the athletes must qualify in one of the many Little Britches Rodeo–sanctioned events. These events are held throughout the country,

The Westernaires are pictured here at the National Western Stock Show around 1970.
Photograph courtesy of Tom Noel Collection

and any rodeo can become a franchise of the Little Britches Rodeo simply by filling out an application and being approved. As of 2003, 180 Little Britches Franchised Rodeos were in existence.

Another Colorado group dedicated to seeing young men and women successful on horseback is the Westernaires. While it is not a rodeo club, this group is dedicated to promoting the knowledge of horsemanship to a group that is not usually associated with a rural lifestyle. It was founded in 1949 with the goal of getting nine- to nineteen-year-olds who live in Jefferson County back to their rural roots of the not-so-distant past. This group maintains its headquarters, Fort Westernaire, adjacent to the Jefferson County Fair Grounds in Golden, Colorado, with two indoor arenas and one outdoor arena, classrooms, and stables for its multitude of horses. As youngsters progress through the program from Tenderfoots, who are the rookies, they can perfect their skills and eventually join many elite performance groups such as the Precisionettes or the Red Cavalry. The Westernaires is dedicated not only to the precision of its drill team, but also to the standards of its members. The group does not allow drug, alcohol, or tobacco use of any kind by participants; instead, it emphasizes teamwork, the shared Western heritage of Colorado, and animal care. In fact, each Westernaire is provided with a rule book that outlines everything from the procedure to rent horses to the dress

Paul McDonald's
Country Studio
Dolores, Colo.
1979 Colorado State High School Finals

Above This high school cowboy is competing in the 1979 Colorado State High School Finals in Durango, Colorado, in the bareback contest. *Photograph courtesy of Earl Barnes*

Right High school rodeos can be just as dangerous as a PRCA rodeo. This student is attempting to crawl away from his bull at a 1980 contest in Henderson, Colorado. *Photograph courtesy of Earl Barnes*

Above High school rodeos take place all over the state and allow students to develop their skills, compete for prizes, and possibly receive rodeo scholarships to colleges around the country. *Photograph courtesy of Earl Barnes*

Left A calf attempts to escape its roper at a high school rodeo competition. *Photograph courtesy of Stephanie Seifried*

Above This high school saddle bronc rider will need to stay out of the mud for at least eight seconds in order to receive a score for his ride. *Photograph courtesy of Stephanie Seifried*

Right High school cowboys are killing time around the horses they will be riding later in the day. One cowboy appears to have already been tossed into the mud. *Photograph courtesy of Stephanie Seifried*

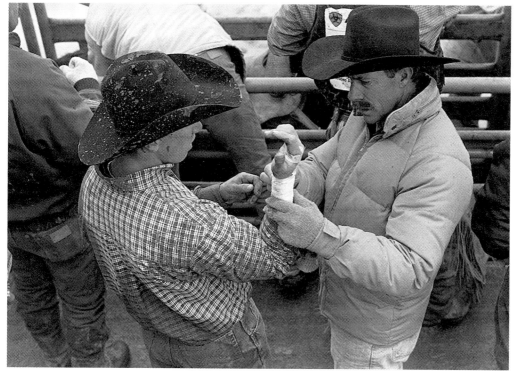

Above These cowboys are saddling a horse at a high school rodeo in Golden, Colorado. *Photograph courtesy of Stephanie Seifried*

Left An injured cowboy is a common sight at any level. This high school competitor has his wrist examined by an adult sponsor. *Photograph courtesy of Stephanie Seifried*

This sign advertises the 2004 Colorado State High School Rodeo Association Finals Rodeo, which was held at the Jefferson County Fair Grounds. *Photograph by Mathew Staver*

codes, which are very detailed for both the boys and girls and are based on levels achieved in the group.

This is a very hardworking bunch of students that holds many events throughout the year to keep its members in top shape, always preparing for the next event and raising money. The Westernaires is a nonprofit group that maintains a rather large number of horses for its members, many of whom do not have the resources to own a horse. The feeding of these animals requires a lot of money, and members pay only a small fee each year. Therefore, the organization holds many fundraising events that members must work either as performers or as behind-the-scenes help. The money raised by this group goes a long way. Westernaires have been competing at the National Western Stock Show since the early 1950s; in 2004, they performed the tricks of the Russian Cossacks as the audience watched these young men jumping from horse to horse with bated breath. In 1997, they were given an opportunity to perform for the leaders of the world, including former President Clinton, when the Summit of the Eight was held in Denver.

School-age children were not the only ones who needed to perfect their skills in the ring, so the idea of the college rodeo was born. College rodeo officially began in 1948 when representatives from twelve colleges met in Texas to form a governing board for their sport, the National Intercollegiate Rodeo

High school students wait to enter the indoor arena at the Jefferson County Fair Grounds. *Photograph courtesy of Stephanie Seifried*

Association (NIRA). The first official meeting of the NIRA was held in Denver, April 14–15, 1949, where the constitution for collegiate rodeo was approved. The constitution dealt with issues ranging from the rodeo structure to the academic eligibility requirements for the athletes, who were to be students first. Colleges from Colorado, Texas, Wyoming, and three other states would create thirteen teams that would then compete against other teams within a set region, allowing for these cowboys and cowgirls to develop their skills for the professional rodeo circuit while ideally working on a degree at the same time. At the end of the first season, a national championship event was held to see who the top college rodeo cowboys were.

College rodeo wouldn't really begin to hit its stride until the 1960s. In 1962, ABC's Wide World of Sports featured the National College Rodeo Finals, and by 1967, ninety-seven schools were members of the NIRA. Many of those schools were two-year junior colleges, not four-year universities. The 1970s saw quite a few changes as rodeo moved into the modern world. Computers were being used to determine rankings. College rodeo also saw the advent of corporate sponsorship for their amateur competitions. College rodeo is still very popular today, and many colleges offer rodeo scholarships that include stipends for boarding horses along with providing fees and tuition for student-athletes. Today, the NIRA puts on over one hundred

A high school cowboy carries his saddle through the snow and mud at the Jefferson County Fair Grounds in April 2004. *Photograph courtesy of Stephanie Seifried*

Opposite

Top These high school rodeo cowboys wait around the chutes at the Jefferson County Fair Grounds in April 2004. *Photograph courtesy of Stephanie Seifried*

Bottom These horses stand ready for their riders at a high school rodeo event. *Photograph courtesy of Stephanie Seifried*

rodeos a year within its various regions, and the program has seen many famous athletes pass through its competitions, such as Ty Murray who worked his way up from the Little Britches to College Champion to World Champion.

Here in Colorado, the first intercollegiate rodeo was held in Boulder at the University of Colorado in April of 1961. Participants came from fifteen different universities to hone their skills and compete for the honor of their respective schools. These college rodeos would not just be limited to four-year universities either. In 1972, Arapahoe Community College, which was a member of the National Intercollegiate Rodeo Association, started its own invitational rodeo named after a local cowboy, Red Fenwick, who, at the time, was writing a column for the *Denver Post*. The Fenwick Stampede took place annually in April, with nineteen colleges from the central Rocky Mountain region competing, including rodeo powerhouses Colorado State University and Casper (Wyoming) College. Unfortunately, college rodeos are waning in the twenty-first century. In 2003, the Northeastern Junior College in Sterling, Colorado, was forced to disband because of higher education budget cuts at the state level. The program could not continue without enough money to support itself.

Colleges were not the only schools that were promoting rodeo as an extracurricular activity. High schools in Colorado also were forming rodeo teams. In fact, there exists both a National High School Rodeo Association (NHSRA) and a Colorado High School Rodeo Association (CHSRA). High school rodeo got its start in 1947 in Hallettsville, Texas, with one hundred students competing that year. The mission of high school rodeo, according to the NHSRA Web site, is "to encourage youth to stay in school and to promote the highest type of conduct and sportsmanship." These are noble goals to say the least, goals that are echoed by many of the rodeo club sponsors and rodeo parents today.

In 1951, the group became a multistate nonprofit organization. By 1957, the sport was receiving write-ups in *Teen* magazine, and today, the sport boasts twelve thousand members nationally from thirty-nine states and also members from Canada and Australia. In Colorado, the sport of rodeo just keeps on growing. More and more clubs continue to join the Colorado High School Rodeo Association; Valley Rodeo Club, founded in 1997, is one of the

Stock contractors serve high school rodeos as well as the National Finals Rodeo. This cowboy looks at the stock for the Valley Rodeo Clubs High School Rodeo in April 2004. *Photograph courtesy of Stephanie Seifried*

latest. Today, high school students compete in events ranging from bull riding (with a signed release form from parents, of course) to pole bending and goat tying for the ladies.

The Colorado High School Rodeo Association is in an uncomfortable position when it comes to liability versus personal responsibility. The CHSRA is a mostly volunteer organization, and it lacks the power and the inclination to tell parents that an injured student cannot compete, except in the cases of injuries that are too big and visible to ignore. Injury and rodeo go hand in hand; however, many cowboys refuse to listen to a well-meaning medical professional when it comes to things like taking time off to recover properly. The CHSRA also has not made safety gear such as helmets mandatory; its members are waiting for the entire culture to change, and this is gradually happening. In the meantime, high school students from all over the state continue to compete.

Jay Sear, age fifteen, from Arvada, Colorado, has been riding since she was eight months old. Today, she is a member of the Lazy Lopers 4-H Club and participates in events from pole bending to calf roping. She even rode a bull once—just for fun and just for two seconds. She has gained a lot from

This bull awaits a rider at a Colorado High School Rodeo Association event in April 2004. *Photograph courtesy of Stephanie Seifried*

her experiences in the CHSRA. She enjoys the traveling even though it can be difficult to balance school and rodeo. She often ends up doing homework in between events to keep her grades up. Not all rodeo clubs have eligibility requirements, but for Jay's mother to allow her to compete, her grades have to meet certain standards. This is a sport that requires discipline, both in and out of the arena. Jay is also responsible for the care of her seven horses. She goes from school to the boarding stables to groom the horses that she rides in her competitions. In short, she is always on the move, which personifies the sport.

Here in Colorado, teams from various schools and areas, twenty-one in all, meet and compete at high school events. These students are also working to hone their skills for the professional rodeos. Teams such as the Bear Creek Rodeo Club and the Ute Mountain High School Rodeo Club, along with quite a few independents, are at these events looking for college scholarships to propel them to the next level. Like their college rodeo counterparts, at the end of the year, a champion must be chosen, and like professional rodeo, points determine the champion. Events take place all over the state throughout the school year, with the ultimate goal being the National High School

While not quite a belt buckle, this young mutton buster seems very proud of his ribbon prize from the Elizabeth Stampede. *Photograph courtesy of the Blakesley family*

Below This young cowboy is attempting to tie up an unco-operative goat. Goat tying trains young participants for calf and steer roping later on in their rodeo careers. *Photograph courtesy of Therese Mousel*

Above A small boy struggles to control his uncooperative horse at the August 2003 rodeo in Hayden, Colorado. *Photograph courtesy of Matthew Meason*

Below Ethan Cook seems to be having problems with his mutton as he hangs on backwards at the Rim Rock in Fruita, Colorado, 2003. *Photograph courtesy of Jim Cook*

Cheylin Corman barrel races in August 2003, developing her skills for the next level of rodeo. *Photograph courtesy of Terry White*

Below left This young barrel racer shows her patriotism on a horse wearing red, white, and blue at the WDS Junior Rodeo in Eaton, Colorado, in August 2003. *Photograph courtesy of Emily Beaton*

Below This cowboy participates in the flag stick competition at the August 2003 WDS Junior Rodeo in Eaton, Colorado. *Photograph courtesy of Emily Beaton*

Black cowboys are making a comeback. This young man is a participant in the Colorado High School Rodeo Association. *Photograph courtesy of Stephanie Seifried*

Below Amber Haugen, age fifteen, is attempting to catch a calf in a 4-H–sponsored contest at the El Paso County Fair in 2003. All she has to do now is convince the calf to cross a finish line. *Photograph courtesy of Autumn Haugen*

At the Little Britches Youth Association Rodeo in Kiowa, Colorado, in 2003, a young boy participates in the pee wee goat tying event. It appears that the goat is winning. *Photograph courtesy of Steve Beaber*

Below Mutton busting is one of the cutest events at a rodeo. Here, the busters try to keep up with some of the rodeo clowns after a grueling competition. The winner, who had to be physically pulled off of his sheep by a clown, got to kiss a rodeo queen as well as take home a trophy almost as big as he was. All contestants on all nights of this event received trophies from Frontier Airlines who sponsored the event. *Photograph by the author*

Above Girls can be just as tough as boys. Katie Porshall won the pee wee calf riding buckle at the Adams County Fair of 2003, beating out seven boys, and she looked good doing it in her leopard print chaps. *Photograph courtesy of Cindy Arndt*

Right A breakaway junior roper participates in the 2003 Yuma County Fair. It looks like he might just get his calf. *Photograph courtesy of Pat Armagost*

Boys aren't the only ones who ride bulls. Here, a young lady is attempting to ride a baby bull in the junior event at the August 2003 Yuma County Fair. *Photograph courtesy of Pat Armagost*

This bike-helmet-wearing cowboy is riding a baby bull at the 2003 Yuma County Fair. *Photograph courtesy of Pat Armagost*

This high school rodeo participant wears a helmet to prevent injury during his bull riding event. *Photograph courtesy of Stephanie Seifried*

Rodeo Finals. A complex system uses an athlete's top ten rodeo perform- ances, plus the first state finals round, plus the second state finals round, plus the championship round, plus the average points of an individual's top ten rodeos. The top four finishers compete in a national competition held each year while finishers five through ten qualify for the Silver State Rodeo.

However, it is much simpler to qualify for the state finals in Colorado. According to Valley Club Rodeo sponsor Tom Bashline, all a student has to do to participate in the state finals is compete in two rodeos throughout the course of a season. This is easier than it sounds as every day counts as a rodeo. As long as a student competes in the same event both days of a week- end rodeo, he is eligible for the finals. The CHSRA season runs from August until July of the following year when the High School National Finals Rodeo is held. Competitions are scheduled on four weekends in the fall, but there are no wintertime events. Instead, after breaking for the weather and holi- days, the CHSRA season resumes in the early spring. In the spring, there are ten weekend events plus the state finals. Many high school riders throughout the state will also go to some of the smaller local events during the off-season

Opposite

Top A high school bull rider holds on while fellow students cheer him on for eight seconds. *Photograph courtesy of Stephanie Seifried*

Bottom High school students compete for scholarships to college rodeo teams and for a chance to make it to the PRCA if they are good enough. *Photograph courtesy of Stephanie Seifried*

Some days, you bust the mutton; other days, the mutton busts you. This young cowboy is obviously having a rough day as the sheep runs off victorious at the 2003 Rim Rock Rodeo in Fruita, Colorado. *Photograph courtesy of Jim Cook*

Below Karlee Wager, age ten, ties her goat at the LaJunta Kids Rodeo in August 2002 while a judge signals in the background once the task has been completed. *Photograph courtesy of Patsy Tompkins*

to try to make some money on the side. The power of that money can be very seductive to these young men and women of the rodeo world.

When riders turn eighteen, they qualify for the Professional Rodeo Cowboys Association (PRCA). This leaves a few of the best cowboys with a big decision to make. They can decide to go on to a college rodeo team, especially if they have a scholarship offer. This route allows them to get an education—something to live off of once their rodeo careers are over. Or they can go directly to the big money and uncertainty of the pros. It is a trade-off one way or the other, and only the individual can decide which choice is right for him. There are no guarantees in the rodeo world, save one. You will get hurt; the only questions are when, where, and how badly.

Chance Tate, of Cortez, Colorado, a high school rodeo participant, was quoted in the December 8, 2003, *Denver Post* as saying, "I rode with a broken pelvis before … a concussion ain't going to hurt much. I plan on making pro. I can't sissy out now." This young man personifies the toughness of the cowboy. He was injured on a Saturday, attended a dance that night, and was riding again on Sunday. High school club sponsor Tom Bashline has seen

A young rodeo fan at the 2004 National Western Stock Show tries to feed one of the horses. *Photograph by the author*

Above Karlee Wager on Hawk runs the poles at the 2002 LaJunta Kids Rodeo. *Photograph courtesy of Patsy Tompkins*

Above right The athletes of rodeo are some of the best in the sports world, and they start at a young age. Here, two cowboys wish each other luck in Collbran, Colorado, at the 1993 Lions Club Junior Rodeo. *Photograph courtesy of Marsha Encke*

Right Jay Sear, a high school rodeo participant, rides her horse Trinket with her young nephew, proving that rodeo is a family affair and that rodeo riders get an early start. *Photograph courtesy of Ginger Sear*

quite a few of his students move on to college rodeo clubs and the pro rodeo circuit. He has even sent a student into the Professional Armed Forces Rodeo Association, which is the rodeo for those fighting for our country.

Another relative newcomer to the rodeo circuit for young competitors is the Colorado Junior Rodeo Association (CJRA), which was founded in 1994. The stated goal of this group is "to provide a quality event allowing youth to advance their rodeo talent in the spirit of fair competition and the appreciation of good sportsmanship." This group gives one thousand youngsters, ages five to eighteen, a chance to compete in mostly timed events. Additionally, the whole family may participate in the Junior Senior team roping event. Here, mom or dad can join the children in the arena to show off roping skills. This organization also has its own finals rodeo in Salida, Colorado, where the fifteen contestants who have won the most money at CJRA-sanctioned events are allowed to compete for $90,000 in prize money in the CJRA Finals. The money is nice, but in the end, these events are about family—passing the tradition of rodeo from grandparents to parents to children.

Many current rodeo sponsors are veterans of the Colorado High School Rodeo Association or the Little Britches. Basin Rodeo Club sponsor Brenda Cundiff notes that she sees many of the people she competed against when she was a contestant in the CHSRA now driving their children to these weekend events. She also feels that this is a great way to spend time with her children. With all of these various levels of rodeo, it is possible for a rider to spend most of his life running from one rodeo to another. In many cases, rodeo is a family affair, keeping everyone on the move for most of the summer and a lot of the rest of the year as well. Bruce Ford, one of the rodeo's more influential cowboys, has fond memories of watching his father compete at the National Western Rodeo and Cheyenne Frontier Days which he shared with *Colorado Country Life:* "I remember sitting there, watching the guys ride, and loving the roar of the crowd. I knew that one day that was where I would be." This shows that rodeo is in the blood in more ways than one, and that rodeo can cycle through the generations. Today, Ford's children compete in rodeo and have become champion riders just like their father. In fact, Royce Ford earned $148,584 in 2003 and finished second at the National Finals Rodeo. Rodeo is a family affair where traditions are passed on, keeping the sport alive and well.

Alternative Cowboys & Cowgirls

RODEO IS A SPORT THAT HAS traditionally been seen as the domain of white male athletes. However, the reality is quite different, and the perceptions of rodeo are not always in sync with reality. While it is true that many of the most famous participants in the sport have been white men, there have also been many contributions by other groups such as Hispanics, Blacks, and women. In fact, the sport of rodeo owes a great debt to all three of these groups for many of its events, such as steer wrestling, and for its traditions. Without the influence of these three groups, the events and culture of rodeo would be very different from the rodeo we know today. Unfortunately, it would take until the second half of the twentieth century for the sport to embrace these overlooked but crucial groups and return rodeo to its ethnic roots in Colorado.

Traditionally, rodeo is a sport with few minorities; however, this tradition has been changing as more and more cowboys of color reclaim their rodeo heritage. The myth of the white West is inaccurate since many cowboys in the Old West were not white. A white West is a belief that is perpetuated by the Hollywood Western. Instead, many of the cowboys in the Old West were

Nat Love, who was also known as "Deadwood Dick," worked as a champion roper for a cattle company and a Pullman porter for a Colorado railroad company. He was born a slave, was freed after the Emancipation Proclamation, and is today one of the most famous black cowboys of the American West. *Photograph courtesy of the Black American West Museum and Heritage Center*

freed slaves who had left their former owners and homes for the wide-open spaces and for opportunities that could not be found in the segregated post–Civil War South that was ruled by Jim Crow Laws and was full of antipathy toward the newly freed. Even more cowboys were of Spanish descent, a culture where the art of the cowboy had begun long before it was adopted by whites looking to become rich off the cattle that lived wild in the West. Yet, both African Americans and Hispanics, with the notable exception of the Pickett brothers and a few others, would spend the early part of the twentieth century estranged from the sport they had helped to create. It would take until the 1970s for rodeo to re-embrace its ethnic roots. Jack Weston writes the following in his book *The Real American Cowboy:*

> Much of the rodeo tradition goes back to sixteenth century Spain. Rodeo culture then traveled to the Americas by way of the migration of many Spanish to the New World who were in the business of raising cattle.
>
> Mexico was at too early a stage of capitalism in the late (eighteen) sixties to develop a cattle industry. And because the Mexicans collected cattle by trapping them in pens around a few watering places or in the brush by tying them to stalking oxen, and because they drove no herd regularly to distant markets, they did not provide all the range and trail methods and skills that Texans were later required to invent.

These early Spanish settlers created the vaquero, the Hispanic version of the cowboy. Early vaqueros would often participate in contests of skill at fiestas, which were usually held at the end of cattle drives. However, these contests were generally only a minor portion of the party; the most important part of the fiesta was the music, dancing, and feasting. Other times, the vaqueros would use these contests to entertain one another on the weekends during long cattle drives. It would take a long time for these early contests to reach a white rodeo audience in Colorado. In fact, many of the events of the sport come from these old Hispanic contests and from the skills that were used by the vaqueros in their daily lives on the trail. In his thesis, "Man, Beast, and Dust," Clifford P. Westermeier states, "For many years in the cattle industry the best ropers were Mexican Vaqueros who moved northward from the Rio Grande and had joined the large cattle outfits." The cattle industry was a natural progression from Hispanic to Anglo culture, driven by supply and demand in the post–Civil War era, and the sport of rodeo was

also a natural progression between the two cultures, one that still permeates rodeo today.

In 1972, a Mexican-style rodeo known as a charreada was held in Denver in conjunction with the formation of the Denver Charro Association. This was a chance for "Mexican-American men to compete in a Latin flavored rodeo," according to a *Rocky Mountain News* article that year. The charreada included many roping events lacking in traditional Anglo rodeos, such as piales en el lienzo, or roping the hind legs of a horse causing him to trip, and the manganas a caballo, the art of tripping a horse with a rope while on horseback. Most of the events at this competition were judged on skill instead of using the clock to determine the winner, and almost half of the events were floreando, or rope art, a marked difference from Americanized rodeo events such as steer wrestling where strength is more important than precision. Of course, as with all aspects of rodeo, animal rights activists did not care for the treatment of the animals by the charros, or cowboys, showing them the same scorn they show rodeos.

The charreada is also filled with events that require strength and skill. The best example of this is the paso de la muerte, the death jump. This is the

The charros line up for the National Anthem at the 2004 National Western Stock Show in Denver. Charros wear army uniforms; therefore, they keep their hats on for the playing of national anthems. *Photograph courtesy of Tom Noel Collection*

A charro rides a bull with two hands at the Mexican Rodeo Extravaganza at the National Western Stock Show in Denver. American cowboys use only one hand. *Photograph courtesy of Tom Noel Collection*

most dangerous of the charro disciplines. Here, a charro jumps from the back of a trained horse onto the back of a wild horse that has never been ridden before. The jumper is aided by his fellow charros, who attempt to guide the wild horse. However, in the end, the charro who is jumping is on his own at the crucial moment; it is only his skill and a little bit of luck that will get him on the back of that untrained second horse. This is a skill that would have been used to catch and tame wild horses in the West more than a hundred years ago. Today, it is a thrilling spectacle for those of us sitting on the edges of our seats and another reminder of a past that should not be forgotten or left behind.

The charro is a proud symbol of the past. The clothing worn by charros is a military uniform, going back to the Mexican Revolution, so charros do not remove their hats during the singing of national anthems, unlike cowboys who do. Charros are also involved in rough stock events such as bareback riding and bull riding; however, even these events differ from their Anglo counterparts. In American rodeo, participants ride until the buzzer sounds after a set number of seconds have passed, depending upon the event. Anglo cowboys only use one hand to hold onto a bucking animal. Charro riders use two hands in the rough stock events. Charros ride until they are either thrown or the horse or bull stops bucking. This can be for a rather long time in the case of some animals, making life difficult for the poor charro who draws a horse with lots of stamina.

By 1976, the popularity of the charreada continued to spread into cities such as Pueblo where the First International Charro Competition was held, August 25–29, 1976. Here, rope art, or floreando, constituted half of the events. Today, charreada can be found at many popular events such as the Colorado State Fair. The National Western Stock Show also joined in the Latin tradition by adding a Mexican Rodeo Extravaganza in 1995. The Extravaganza was the dream of Jerry Diaz, also known as Charro de Corazon, Charro of the Heart. The show began as a small portion of the National Western Stock Show and has only gotten bigger as it has developed. Today, this show is one of the biggest draws at the National Western Stock Show and one of the more unusual shows, featuring a rich cultural tradition that educates many about rodeo's history.

This annual show has presented acts such as Los Zapatistas, a female precision sidesaddle riding team, which is also part of the cultural heritage of Mexico. These women and their horses perform incredible feats, making elaborate patterns and passes that seem to be almost impossible without some accident occurring. Yet, these athletes are so well trained that while the horses may come within fractions of inches of one another, no collisions occur. Other acts at the Extravaganza include Gerardo "Jerry" Diaz, the founder, who is still in charge of his dream project today. Diaz has a number of well-trained horses that perform amazing feats. His act includes anything from horses dancing in time to the music to horses that allow Diaz to take brief naps on their bellies while the horses themselves nap. In this event, it becomes apparent to the biggest city slicker that these horses are something special. Diaz also is a skilled roper who makes his rope, made of the same cactus that is used in making tequila, dance. He can twirl his rope while standing on the back of a galloping horse, which becomes even more impressive when one realizes that he is also twirling the rope around the two of them as they move. The Mexican Rodeo Extravaganza is evidence that rodeo in Colorado has come full circle.

The Extravaganza returns to the original cultural roots of the rodeo with the influence of Mexico and South America. The whole show is set to the sounds of a mariachi band. In fact, charros thrive on the noise of the band and the crowd and ask for applause and encouragement. This is different from a regular rodeo where silence is the norm while the cowboys ply their trade. The announcing at the Mexican Extravaganza is in both English and Spanish, and the show appeals to a wider demographic than the traditional rodeo would. Coverage for the Mexican rodeo appears in English newspapers such as the *Rocky Mountain News* and the *Denver Post*. This rodeo is also covered in *La Voz,* a Spanish publication located in Denver. By 2003, the Mexican Rodeo Extravaganza was one of the more popular shows at the Stock Show and was one of the fastest selling events. It is also a reminder that rodeo is a diverse sport that is derived from many cultures and colors.

The Hispanic influence is not the only one overlooked when one thinks of the sport of rodeo. Another overlooked group that has been very important to rodeo's development is the African American cowboy. In many rodeos, this was a figure that was all but missing in the stands or in the arena. However, in the 1970s, rodeo saw the reemergence of the black cowboy, an often overlooked figure in the Old West of popular culture, but one that had a rather large presence in the reality of the Old West. One of the scouts of the Lewis and Clark Expedition was black, starting a trend that would be overlooked for years. Later in the nineteenth century, many freed slaves would head west after the Civil War to tend to the herds of cattle that were freely roaming the plains. Even before that time, many slaves were already working the range and breaking horses for their masters. They were becoming highly competent cowboys. In 1887, a cowboy tournament was held that pitted white cowboys against black cowboys. Famous cattleman Charles Goodnight was known to trust his black cowhands with the payrolls. History records that he once asked Bose Ikerd to oversee twenty thousand dollars in cash, something unheard of at the time.

However, many of the blacks on the cattle drives were relegated to cooking duties. It would take until the early 1900s for the Pickett brothers, who were black, to bring the idea of the non white cowboy back to life in a rodeo arena, if only for a brief moment. William Pickett was a revolutionary rider who invented bulldogging; he would be one of many black cowboys to grace a rodeo arena. In 1971, Bill Pickett would also be the first to be inducted into the Rodeo Cowboy Hall of Fame. He was the most famous of the black cowboys. The Norman Film Manufacturing Company of Jacksonville, Florida,

Bill Pickett, shown here on horseback, was the first cowboy of color inducted into the Rodeo Hall of Fame. He is also credited with the invention of bulldogging. *Photograph courtesy of the Black American West Museum and Heritage Center*

Above Bass Reeves was a black deputy U.S. marshal in the Indian Territory of Oklahoma for thirty years. He was responsible for rounding up outlaws and bringing them to justice. He died in 1910. *Photograph courtesy of the Black American West Museum and Heritage Center*

Above right Ned Huddleston, also known as Isom Dart, was a black cowboy who lived in Brown's Park in northwestern Colorado. Tom Horn killed him in 1900 after Huddleston refused to leave the predominantly white area. *Photograph courtesy of the Black American West Museum and Heritage Center*

Opposite At the 1916 Bakersfield Rodeo in California, F. Greenway is riding the horse Stampede. Many black cowboys who competed in white rodeos stuck with timed events rather than rough stock events because there was less opportunity for discrimination. *Photograph courtesy of the Black American West Museum and Heritage Center*

produced a film called *The Bull Dogger,* starring Pickett. Teddy Roosevelt once said, "Pickett's name will go down in Western history as being one of the best trained ropers and riders the West has produced."

Bill Pickett is considered by most to be the inventor of bulldogging, also known as steer wrestling. In 1900, at the Arkansas Valley Fair in Rocky Ford, Colorado, Pickett took a life-threatening action in the ring and turned it into a brand new event. Ralph Taylor, a local historian from the 1960s, relates the encounter in a 1969 edition of the *Pueblo Chieftain:* "The Bull tossed Picket overhead, but the cowboy held onto the horns. In effect it was a fall for the bull…. [H]e grabbed the animal's horns again and twisted his neck until the big bull was compelled to fall. This brought cheer from the crowd." Bulldogging was born. There are many different theories why this event is called bulldogging. The most colorful involves Pickett himself. It was believed that Bill Pickett would actually bite the cattle on the lips and ears, similar to the methods used by dogs to herd the cattle, hence the name bulldogging. Pickett was also known for hoolihaning, a term used when a cowboy plants the

E Greenway
on "Stampede"
Bakersfield Rodeo
Sept 1-4 1916

Cowboys adjust their saddle stirrups at the Ted Gage Ranch in Denver at the second Colored Rodeo Association of Denver event in September 1948. *Photograph courtesy of Denver Public Library, Western History Collection x-21934*

horns of the steer into the ground. This is considered to be very dangerous for the steer, and today it is against the rules to plant an animal's horns. Either way, steer wrestling is not an event for the faint of heart. In this event that truly pits man against beast, all competitors must be strong, fast, and fearless to overcome a rather large animal that is usually quite uncooperative.

Since Bill Pickett, bulldogging has become an accepted rodeo practice, both in competition and for fun and entertainment. Another unusual bulldogging incident took place in the old movie towns of Colorado. Around the turn of the century, many Westerns were produced in the state, featuring cowboys turned actors and stuntmen. In 1911, one of the actors, Tom Mix, was spending his free time bulldogging steers from an automobile, as opposed to the traditional horse used in rodeo competition. The incident was recorded in the *Cañon City Record,* and it directly referred to "bulldogging," showing both the spread of the event and the influence of Pickett.

As for the rest of the black cowboys, there would be few chances to compete during the first half of the twentieth century. In 1947, the Negro Cowboys Rodeo Association was formed. This group organized some weekend

Leon Coffee, a black rodeo clown, and his mule Leona are pictured around 1985 at the National Western Stock Show. *Photograph courtesy of Tom Noel Collection*

rodeos for black cowboys. One of the most famous black cowboys from Colorado, Alonzo Pettie, was instrumental in these rodeos. Pettie, born in 1910, began his career on wild bulls and broncs and suffered a series of injuries. At an event in 1929, he injured his shoulder while on a bronc and then, with his arm in a sling, proceeded to ride a bull. He won. In those days, blacks were not allowed to participate in most rodeos. However, they were permitted to entertain the crowd by riding the rough stock animals and being tossed into the dirt. These black cowboys were paid per animal they rode. Pettie remembers, "If you were a good rider, well, you would go ahead and ride … and if you would get bucked off you would get your $2 to $3 or whatever … you could make $10 or $12 a day like that." After a couple of years in the army during World War II, Pettie started the all-black rodeos. These were mostly weekend affairs where black cowboys competed against one another for small amounts of money. Unfortunately for Pettie, he was so severely injured at one of these competitions that his rodeo career was ended forever. He went on to work for the Sears Roebuck Co., and in 1996, he became a Levi's jeans model in the Red Tab Heritage Campaign.

Those weekend rodeos were just the first step in including blacks in the sport of rodeo. In 1968, the Black Cowboys Association was formed, and in 1971, Bill Pickett was inducted into the Rodeo Hall of Fame. There was a smattering of successful black cowboys in the rodeo business during this time, ranging from Charlie Sampson, world champion bull rider and Timex spokesman (which makes sense when you realize that bull riders also "take a licking and keep on ticking") to Leon Coffee, the famous rodeo clown. However, there was no real rodeo emphasis in the black community. That all changed in Denver in 1984 when the late Bill Pickett was honored with an all-black rodeo named after him. The Bill Pickett Invitational Rodeo began its life at the Adams County Fair Grounds that year. Lu Vason, a concert promoter, who turned rodeo buff when he attended Cheyenne Frontier Days in 1977, founded it. Here, Vason noticed that everyone was having a good time, himself included. However, there were no black faces in the crowd or on the horses in the ring.

Thus, an idea was born—that of an all-black rodeo with a mission of educating the world about black cowboys who had been left out of the history books, cowboys such as Bill Pickett. Vason faced some challenges going from concerts to rodeo and learned quite a bit about the intricacies of the sport. Two of the biggest problems he faced were finding a venue for the event and finding stock contractors to ensure that there were animals for the event. The first rodeo was a learning process, but it has proved a successful one that has opened many doors for black cowboys. Today, many successful black cowboys can claim to have received their start at the Bill Pickett Rodeo, and some have even gone on to become world champions, such as Fred Whitfield.

The Bill Pickett Rodeo, first held in 1984, was the first blacks only rodeo in Colorado since the 1940s. Today, the Bill Pickett Invitational Rodeo is America's only touring black rodeo, making stops in cities from Denver to Oakland to Philadelphia. Its events range from bulldogging to ladies steer undecorating where women on horseback must chase down a steer and pull the ribbon off the shoulder. Part of the profits go to the Bill Pickett Memorial Scholarship Fund, which supports young black athletes who are interested in pursuing careers in rodeo. It has also succeeded in getting blacks involved in the sport of rodeo and re-creating a more accurate picture of the Old West, one made up of men and women of all colors.

One of the myths of the Old West is that of the cowboys and Indians fighting with each other. This may have some basis in fact, though many of

A black cowboy is seen waiting for his event to begin at a high school rodeo competition. More and more black cowboys are getting involved with the sport because of events such as the Bill Pickett Rodeo. *Photograph courtesy of Stephanie Seifried*

today's cowboys are Native Americans. The Indians have come full circle, ironically to preserve their heritage. The introduction of the horse into the culture of the tribes of the West was a momentous event. The Spanish conquistadors had introduced these horses; some had escaped to breed in the wild. Later, these wild horses were captured by many of the tribes who tended to name the "exotic" creatures as dogs. The Blackfoot tribe called horses "elk dogs," while the Lakota referred to horses as "holy dogs." The tribes believed that horses were gifts from the Great Spirit, a belief that was reinforced by the absence of white men at this time. In his book *Riders of the West: Portraits from Indian Rodeo,* Peter Iverson expressed a common belief: "With the right horse anything was possible," and with the horse, the nomadic groups flourished, as hunting became easier with the tribes able to move more quickly.

Eventually, the pioneers conquered the tribes, and the passage of the Dawes Act confined the tribes to reservations. Despite the troubles, an outlet for the old ways was being developed in rodeo. Many Indians were able to take their skills on horseback and channel them into the developing sport.

Problems, however, did exist. For instance, many Indians felt that the judges were biased against them, so many who competed stuck with the timed events instead of the rough stock events. There was less likelihood of the clock being biased. Indians also faced problems in leaving the reservations and finding the money for travel and entry fees. Despite this, many Indians did make it in early rodeo. One of the most famous was Will Rogers, who was part Cherokee, and who, incidentally, was a hazer for Bill Pickett. Other famous Indian cowboys were Jackson Sundown of the Nez Perce tribe and Tom Three Persons of the Blood Indian tribe. By 1957, the All Indian Rodeo Cowboys Association was founded. It later became the All Indian Professional Rodeo Cowboys Association (AIPRCA). This group founded schools for both judges and riders; it also worked to promote cultural events, such as powwows, to accompany the rodeo contests. "Being a cowboy seemed to be a good way to remain an Indian." By 1976, the first National Finals Rodeo was held by the AIPRCA at the Salt Palace in Salt Lake City, Utah. Today, the organization has five different regions in Canada and nine different regions in the United States.

Minority groups were not the only ones embracing rodeo. Women also wanted to get in on the action. As America moved into the 1940s, rodeo gained more and more popularity in Colorado. It went from being an almost exclusively male sport to including some female participants. The 1946 presentation of the National Western Stock Show seems to have been a precursor to women competing in timed events and competing for prize money and points alongside their male counterparts. Not only were women competing, but they were also winning the admiration of the crowd. The *Rocky Mountain News* reported: "The crowd had more applause for Miss Sawyer who rose from the tanbark where Belen had thrown her, dusted the dirt from her white riding habit and returned to the saddle to give a masterful exhibition of horse handling."

Three years later, in August 1949, the first all-girls rodeo was held in Denver. Some of the events were ones that could typically be found at male rodeos, events such as steer riding, calf roping, and bronco riding. The women had a few events that were uniquely their own, such as wild cow milking, western pleasure riding, western trail horse riding, and the cloverleaf race. Today, the cloverleaf race is better known as barrel racing, a sport in which only the ladies compete.

The first all-girls rodeo had moments that were full of excitement, such as when Miss Shirley Chafin was taken to Denver General with the broken

Above Dancing horses at the National Western Stock Show were the original entertainment until the debut of the rodeo in 1931. Women dominated this event. *Photograph courtesy of Tom Noel Collection*

Far left Chelsey Wager and her horse Joe run the barrels at the LaJunta Kids Rodeo in 2002. *Photograph courtesy of Patsy Tompkins*

Left Shirly Tate, nine, and Monica Matlock, twelve, participated and placed in several events, including barrel racing, at the horse show in Meeker, Colorado, in 2003. *Photograph courtesy of Marlene Tate*

Toni Strandberg and her horse Dip are racing around the Flying Heels Arena in Granby in the 2003 barrel racing event. *Photograph courtesy of Geneva Cohn*

Right Here, a barrel racer participates in the Ski Hi Stampede Rodeo. A barrel racer is only as good as her horse, and barrel racers invest a lot of time and money in their horses. *Photograph courtesy of Lisa Sieg*

ribs she had suffered in the cloverleaf race. Other events were not nearly as exciting; not a single calf was roped. Sunny Webschall of Golden was overheard saying, "Hey, call time. We can't run that steer to death." Other girls rodeos were a bit more action-packed, although not always in good ways. The first all-girls rodeo held in Colorado Springs had more than its fair share of mishaps. Out of forty-five entrants, Frances Wees of Big Springs, Texas, was knocked unconscious while Eddie Moore of Long Beach, California, was almost totally thrown from her horse, as reported by the *Colorado Springs Gazette*. Only her boot managed somehow to stay in the stirrup. In all, two accidents out of forty-five is fairly good odds, and these all-girls rodeos were the beginning of what would eventually become the Women's Professional Rodeo Association (WPRA).

Women were also able to show their skills in the 1952 National Western Stock Show, which was to be the biggest in National Western history. Some spectators came to see the new Denver Coliseum while others came for the entertainment and the spectacle of the horse show and rodeo just as they had always done. With the new Coliseum came new thrills as well. Two famous female trick riders who had performed in Hollywood, Shirley and Sharron Lucas, were scheduled to perform that year. These two women were famous for their death-defying stunts performed while on horseback. Stunts included "suicide drags," in which the women would be dragged behind the horses, and "split to the neck" and the "hippodrome stand," both of which defy description. All of these stunts were guaranteed to wow audiences and to showcase the talents of women riders in an era when many women stayed at home.

The girls of the rodeo would start slow and work their way toward equality. One of the ways they did this was through developing their natural talent and skills on horseback. In 1963, an eleven-year-old girl competed in the barrel racing competition at the National Western Stock Show Rodeo. Candice Merritt, the talented barrel racer, was competing in her first year as a working member of the Girls Rodeo Association. This group was founded in 1948 with seventy-four original members and has since morphed into the WPRA with over two thousand members. Of course, rodeo was still considered a man's world, and women have been trying to catch up ever since, even if it meant not competing.

At the 1985 National Western Stock Show, the women took a stand. They protested their status as compared with that of the men. Barrel racers refused to race, citing unequal pay. The National Western was offering the women $10,000, up from $7,500 the previous year, but the women were

Barrel racing is the most obvious place for women to compete at PRCA-sanctioned events such as the Greeley Stampede. Women also have their own rodeos under the Women's Professional Rodeo Association (WPRA). *Photograph courtesy of the Chesney family*

demanding $17,000. Women argued that barrel racing was one of the most expensive sports in rodeo because of the costs of their animals, which are crucial to the event, and the cost of the rest of their equipment. They wanted a more equal share of the prize money to make up for this, and when that was denied, they ended up boycotting the rodeo that year. The women returned in 1986, after the National Western met their demands for the $17,000 in prize money.

The National Western was actually behind the curve when it came to treating women as equals. Coors Brewing Company of Golden, Colorado, which had been sponsoring the Chute Out series of rodeos throughout the country, was the first to pay a bonus stipend to the female barrel racers. This extra cash would put the women's prize money on a par with what the men were earning. Coors has sponsored female as well as male rodeo stars. The most famous barrel racer, Charmayne James, with lifetime earnings of

Cedar Dowis, the Kit Carson County Rodeo Queen for 2002, has the honor of carrying the flag of the United States during the playing of the National Anthem. Rodeo queens must be very adept on horseback. *Photograph courtesy of Terry White*

$1.9 million and eleven world championships, was one of Coors' many endorsees until she retired from the world of rodeo to become a mother. Although, even today, barrel racing is the most obvious rodeo event for female competitors, within the WPRA, women can compete in many of the events that men do. They may also be rodeo queens, ambassadors of the sport of rodeo.

The rodeo queen programs throughout the country are another way that women participate in rodeo. In Colorado, the rodeo queen Miss Rodeo Colorado is chosen during the Fourth of July celebration at the Rocky Mountain Stampede, formerly known as the Greeley Independence Stampede. She then represents the state at events such as the PRCA National Finals Rodeo in Las Vegas and makes many appearances throughout Colorado, such as at the National Western Stock Show. Many rodeo queens, such as the Colorado State High School Rodeo Queen, get their start at smaller rodeos and work

This cowgirl has just completed her run through the barrels and is returning to the finish line at the Meeker Range Call and Rodeo, July 4, 2003. *Photograph courtesy of Sharon Bradshaw*

their way up to the big time with the ultimate goal of becoming Miss Rodeo America. Besides the title and prestige, the winner of this contest also receives a ten-thousand-dollar college scholarship.

Rodeo queens have a unique role in rodeo culture. Their clothes, which can be purchased at specialty stores, denote their status as rodeo queens. They also have clinics and camps to help them train to become rodeo queens. According to the rodeo queen Web site, queens are judged in three areas. The first is appearance; an aspiring rodeo queen must look the part of a western girl. Pants and western-style shirts are the norm. Second, contestants are judged on personality; they show off their knowledge of the rodeo world and current events. Last, but certainly not least, is horsemanship. This is the most crucial part of the formula. Rodeo queens make many appearances on horseback in parades and also escort the winners of various rodeo events around the arena for a victory lap. The ability to ride is important for any good rodeo queen, and potential queens will draw unknown horses, just like the men in rough stock events do. Stock contractors provide these horses, and the women then have the opportunity to display their skills on their unfamiliar horses for the judges. Finally, rodeo queens must meet the following two requirements: They must have never been married, and they must be under the age of twenty-four.

All of these groups have come a long way to take their place in the sport of rodeo, and each group brings unique qualities to a sport once regarded as the domain of white males. Time, however, marches on, and nothing remains the same. Those old traditions are changing, allowing for rodeo to reach new groups of people, from city slickers to minorities to girls. After all, the sport of rodeo is a significant part of our history, and it is important to acknowledge the contributions of all groups.

Above Girls involved in rodeo have to learn to take a tumble and keep going. Be it the mutton busting event or bull riding, women are getting more involved in rodeo in the twenty-first century. *Photograph courtesy of Jim Cook*

Left Miss Rodeo America's horse is all dressed up waiting for the show to begin at the 2004 National Western Stock Show in Denver. *Photograph by the author*

Below A rodeo queen moves quickly out of the Denver Coliseum after a rodeo performance at the 2004 Western Stock Show. Rodeo queens, the ambassadors of rodeo, are judged on appearance, personality, and horsemanship. *Photograph by the author*

Modern-day Cows & Cowpokes

RED FENWICK ONCE SAID, "I can't decide which way I like rodeo better—the old time, bare-knuckle, hell-bent-for-payday competition it used to be or the more sophisticated, records-keeping sport that it has become." The man had a point, as rodeo has changed with the times. It has come a long way from Deer Trail, Colorado, and that early cowboy contest, or even before that momentous occasion, when men rode the range betting on each other's skills to kill time. Yet from its simple origins on the trail, rodeo has evolved into a modern form of entertainment for a modern audience. It has gone from daylight competitions in the great outdoors of the West to indoor laser light shows complete with a techno remix of the *Bonanza* theme song and pyrotechnics, which illustrate just how far the sport has come. Today, rock-and-roll music is as likely to play as classic country music; in fact rock-and-roll seems to be the preference these days.

Cowboys have also experienced a revolution right along with their sport. The image of the lone drifter of the plains who might let off some steam when he hits the end of the trail at various unsavory establishments has been gradually replaced by families driving from rodeo to rodeo with equipment

This bull rider at the 2003 Meeker Range Call hangs on for eight seconds. Bull riders have the highest injury rates of all rodeo competitors by a substantial margin. *Photograph courtesy of Glen Bishard*

Here, barriers divide the athletes from the spectators. This is where the rodeo contestants enter the Denver Coliseum for their events at the National Western Stock Show. *Photograph by the author*

and horses in tow. These men and women take their sport very seriously, as well they should. They work just as hard as those toiling away on the gridiron or the basketball court. Taking their sport as seriously as other athletes, they have started to train for their competitions as any other athlete might do, although this has been a slower change than the promoters might like to admit. Safety is also taken seriously as more and more bull riders are wearing protective helmets and vests, which were developed in 1993. "Tuff" Hedemen, a former-bull-rider-turned-rodeo-promoter, ponders how bull riders survive: "What surprises me is that more people don't die." When one is up against an animal that is ten times the size of the average cowboy, some safety gear seems to make a lot of sense. For bull riders, it was easy to incorporate safety vests into the cowboy culture, as they look and fit like a Western-style vest. The vests can be worn while the bull riders keep their image as tough athletes who fear nothing, which can't be far from the truth. They also incur fewer injuries which logically allows for more performances and more money. A vest is a good investment, but it can only do so much. While vests help protect internal organs from the stomping of a one-ton bull, every so often a bull does get in a lucky shot. When leaving the chute, it is just the rider against the bull, "and the bulls do not care."

A cowboy and a bronc go by in a blur at the 2004 National Western Stock Show Rodeo. This particular cowboy was the winner that day. *Photograph by Mathew Staver*

Below A bucking bronc kicks up mud and heaven knows what else at a rodeo held after a snowstorm in April. *Photograph courtesy of Stephanie Seifried*

The Professional Bull Riders, competing against the PRCA's Xtreme Bulls Tour, market themselves as the world's first extreme sport with a $1 million top prize at their national championships. Those in the know refer to bull riding as "the most dangerous eight seconds in sports," and a series of articles that appeared in the *Denver Post* in December 2003 supports them: "The percentage of 'exposures' resulting in injury for rough stock events ... is five times greater than football, more than six times greater than wrestling, and more than 12 times greater than ice hockey." In short, the sport is dangerous, which is part of the appeal. Despite these statistics, it has been harder to convince these same cowboys who wear vests that helmets are also an important piece of safety equipment, although you do see more and more cowboys giving up their hats in favor of preventing concussions. Wiley Peterson, one of the top riders on the PBR, wears one. "You can hang on to tradition and lose your teeth, or lose some tradition and keep your teeth.... [T]his is an extreme sport, and it's moving away from the cowboy feel to it."

Despite this gradual shift, the greatest obstacle to safety would have to be the cowboy culture itself. Bull riders of the past wore cowboy hats, and the cowboys of the present seem slow to embrace the change to helmets, despite the fact that 12 percent of all bull riding injuries are concussions. One of the first steps toward helmets began with World Champion Charlie Sampson, who, after being seriously injured in a command performance for the president, was forced to wear a lacrosse helmet with mask to prevent further injury and death. Today, that particular helmet can be viewed at the Pro

Left Rodeo gear, consisting of bags and saddles, is strewn on the ground. Soon, the contestants will come back and claim their belongings before the night's competition at the 2004 National Western Stock Show. *Photograph by the author*

Right This rodeo clown-in-training is poised to help in Brush, Colorado, 2003. He already has the look down. Suspenders, baggy pants, and loud socks make the man in this profession. Rodeo clowns are an important part of rodeo. *Photograph courtesy of Sandy Kane*

Rodeo Hall of Fame. Unfortunately, wearing a helmet is a rare occurrence, even today. Many cowboys feel that wearing a helmet slows down their reaction times and makes them more vulnerable to injury because of the false confidence this equipment provides. This is complicated by the fact that these early helmets are just modified hockey helmets, which are lighter than the original. These helmets do help with some head trauma, but not all serious head injuries in bull riding are going to be prevented with a mere helmet. That is just a fact of life for bull riders.

In 1981, the Justin Boots Company sponsored a study to track rodeo injuries. Today, they have compiled a database from the last twenty-plus years that allows for better treatment of injuries, which lets cowboys get back into the arena more quickly. Another group of researchers at West Texas A&M University has found that those who compete in rodeo have an 89 percent chance of being injured over the course of a season; in comparison, college football players have only a 47 percent chance of injury. For the cowboy, getting in and out of physical therapy quickly is imperative to having a successful and lucrative career. These statistics are all well and good, but what of the

Judging can be a difficult task, especially for the official in the arena with action. Judges are responsible for evaluating both the cowboy and the animal. PRCA judges are also required to be aware of the condition of the animals they judge. In this photo, the judge is ducking away from the action at the 2003 Elizabeth Stampede. *Photograph courtesy of Jodie Mooney*

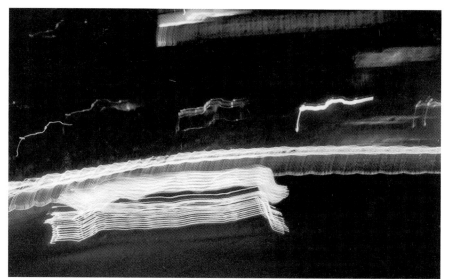

Above Jimmy Schumacher, a retired rodeo clown, is pictured with Willard E. Simms at the 1971 National Western Stock Show. *Photograph by Don Colao, courtesy of Tom Noel Collection*

Above right Here, a Westernaire rides through a darkened Denver Coliseum as part of the opening ceremony for the National Western Stock Show Rodeo in 2004. One of the riders carried an American flag made up entirely of red, white, and blue colored lights. *Photograph by the author*

Right These horses peer out of their trailer waiting for their turn at a high school rodeo in Golden, Colorado. Horses travel all around the country in these trailers. *Photograph courtesy of Stephanie Seifried*

Below The PBR made a stop in Colorado Springs in April of 2003. This high-tech opening ceremony illustrates how far rodeo has come from its start in 1869 in Deer Trail, Colorado. *Photograph courtesy of Sandra Kelch*

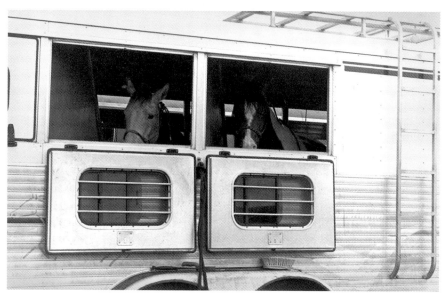

Even mutton busters need a helping hand. A young mutton fighter is poised to give aid should the rider tumble from her sheep in the Rollin' H Arena in Brush, Colorado, August 2003. *Photograph courtesy of Sandy Kane*

Below left An ironic sign located at the Jefferson County Fair Grounds lets people know they need to find a different door to get their horses into the building. *Photograph courtesy of Stephanie Seifried*

Below The only figure in focus is the cowboy hanging on to his bronc at the 2004 National Western Stock Show. *Photograph by Mathew Staver*

Above Here, cowboys are shown warming up their saddles in preparation for their events at the 2004 National Western Stock Show. *Photograph by Mathew Staver*

Right A young cowboy tries his luck on the mechanical bull. These "bulls" are set to the ability of the rider. The better you are, the harder they buck. *Photograph by author*

SOUTH FORK '97

Above Bull fighters are responsible for protecting riders once they are free of the animal. Horses cannot be used because they are vulnerable to the charging of an angry bull. *Photograph courtesy of Stacy Cline*

Left This bull rider wears a helmet, which may go against tradition but helps prevent head injuries, some of the most common and most devastating injuries that plague bull riders. *Photograph courtesy of Lisa Sieg*

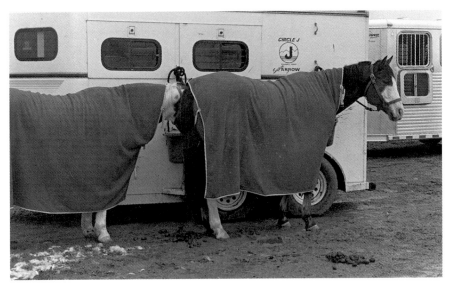

Above Jace Christian watches the action, looking like a smaller version of an authentic cowboy. *Photograph courtesy of Cindy Andt*

Above right Rodeo is a dangerous sport, and cowboys are often seriously injured. This Air Life of Greeley helicopter transports a patient from the Earl Anderson Memorial Rodeo in Grover, Colorado, in 2003. *Photograph courtesy of Lee Bender*

Center Rodeo is a sport that tends to be vulnerable to the elements, as most rodeos are held outdoors. This means that both humans and horses have to find ways to stay warm. These horses are bundled up on a snowy Saturday in April of 2004. *Photograph courtesy of Stephanie Seifried*

Right This cowboy is wearing a protective vest and a lot of mud, having just completed his ride at the Jefferson County Fair Grounds in April 2004. *Photograph courtesy of Stephanie Seifried*

stoic culture of the cowboy? One can assume that not all injuries are reported; in fact, it is highly likely that serious competitors ignore many of the lesser injuries. A typical cowboy attitude, according to one orthopedic surgeon, is, "I had two six-packs and it still hurts. What do I do?" Cowboys will often compete injured because they can. Royce Ford once competed with a broken foot; he simply went out and bought a boot that would fit after his injury caused the foot to swell three sizes. He may have been forced to use crutches to get around, but one doesn't need to be able to walk to ride a bronc. If the cowboys don't compete, they can't win, and without winning, they can't make any money. Although the attitude of cowboys toward the medical profession is changing, it is going to be slow going, as part of the appeal of the sport is its inherent danger. Part of the challenge facing health-care professionals who help the cowboys are the cowboys themselves.

It is that danger and adrenaline rush that has given rise to an unusual phenomenon, the bull riding school. Larry Lancaster operates the Rock-N-Roll Rodeo School out of Arvada, Colorado, which also instructs interested students in bull fighting. Lancaster caters mostly to men aged fifteen to twenty-five, with a few women signing on, but not many. The school allows the rookies to ride smaller bulls, usually weighing between two hundred to seven hundred pounds less than the bulls used in competition. These bulls also tend to buck less than those used by professional bull riders. While the bulls are smaller, the thrill remains the same, although safety regulations at the school are much tougher than those of the PRCA. The school provides all protective gear such as vests, helmets, and protective braces for the neck and back. The school focuses on proper techniques to help keep its clientele safe and coming back for more. Instructors also train students in the art of bull fighting. Bull fighters are an integral part of keeping the riders safe once they are off the bull, the "first line of defense," according to official PRCA documents. They are responsible for distracting the bull from the often-disoriented rider. These men must be very athletic as they are constantly leaping out of harm's way and the bull's reach.

These amateur cowboys are merely weekend warriors when compared to real working cowboys who also compete in their own rodeos. The Working Ranch Cowboys Association (WRCA) is a group that is "preserving the heritage and lifestyle of the Working Ranch Cowboy." This group was founded in 1995 to promote the rodeo skills of real-life ranch hands in the modern world. While these men and women may not be competing in the PRCA, they are athletes in their own right. These are the men and women

still living the lifestyle that gave birth to rodeo. In fact, only ranch owners or those employed on a working ranch may join the WRCA; on occasion, exceptions are made based on unemployment caused by range conditions. Members pay dues based on their status at the ranch, with cowboys paying less than owners would. The WRCA has its own sanctioned rodeos in Hugo, Colorado, and Colorado Springs, Colorado, and it also has its own World Championship Rodeo. The WRCA differs from the PRCA in that its events are tailored to the skills needed by a working cowboy.

In the Ranch Horse Show, a WRCA event, a contestant and his horse must complete a set of skills within a five-minute time limit, ranging from boxing in a cow to roping a cow to how quickly the horse can perform certain key maneuvers. On occasion, a rerun will be granted, but, according to the official rule book, this is "only given if the cow is blind, crippled, insane, or leaves the arena working floor." In other words, this is a rather rare occurrence. Contestants are both scored and timed, and only the most competent cowboys and cowgirls can win. Other contests include chasing and saddling wild horses, mock branding calves, and milking wild horses.

Another type of rodeo that is often overlooked is the Weekend Rodeo. These rodeos are held for tourists in mountain towns throughout the state, such as Steamboat Springs and Winter Park. Not a recent development, they have been around almost as long as rodeo itself, when locals would compete for a quick twenty bucks. "Those were the days when some guys, not your typical cowboys but people from the ski area, would maybe have a beer or two and bet on a bull on a dare," reminisces J. C. Trujillo of Steamboat, who was an elite bareback rider before he retired. Weekend Rodeos are a great way to introduce a new audience to an already growing sport, a sport that has some of the most well-mannered athletes in the world.

Rodeo riders look out for each other. The WRCA is dedicated to its Cowboy Crisis Fund, which helps cowboys and their families in times of need. This can happen quite a bit on the rodeo circuit. There are many groups that also exist to help the cowboy. HealthSouth, a physical therapy group, donates its resources to aid injured cowboys while others hire cowboys for less dangerous and less thrilling work that looks much better than "bronc buster" on an application for health insurance. Cowboys have a short career in which to find their fortune, and many will

This wild milking team is actually managing to milk its cow at the Ride for the Brand Rodeo in Penrose Stadium, Colorado Springs, Colorado, July 2003. This event is a Working Ranch Cowboys Association Rodeo that is only open to cowboys working on active ranches. *Photograph courtesy of Diane G. Erickson*

Facing page

Top This bull fighter at the 2003 Elizabeth Stampede runs in to distract the animal from the recently thrown cowboy, who is most likely disoriented and very vulnerable. *Photograph courtesy of Jodie Mooney*

Bottom These clowns rush to protect a cowboy at the 2003 Greeley Independence Stampede. The rodeo clowns have a huge responsibility, protecting cowboys by diverting the bulls toward themselves. *Photograph courtesy of Emily Beaton*

Right This cowboy takes care of his horse so his horse can take care of him. A horse is an investment, and those who compete in rodeos take care of these creatures. *Photograph courtesy of Emily Beaton*

Below Those who work the chutes are an important part of rodeo. Here, Gene Nelson on the gates and Brian Nussbaum on the long rope prepare to let the excitement begin at the Earl Anderson Memorial Rodeo in June 2000. *Photograph courtesy of Kirk Rush*

Wishing each other good luck before an event, these two young men are part of a long tradition of good sportsmanship and helping out a fellow cowboy. *Photograph courtesy of Marsha Encke*

turn to agents to arrange endorsement deals that can also pull a cowboy family through a tight spot after an injury. The PBR also has set aside money from its television revenues to help its injured bull riders and their families until they get back on their feet and back on the bulls.

Cowboys only get paid if they enter and win. No guarantees exist in rodeo, and helping one another out is one of the basic tenets of the cowboy, out of necessity more than anything else. Cowboys who have enough to make it to a particular rodeo may lack the resources to pay for a hotel room. Cowboy Bruce Ford recalls, "There were times I [slept] in a sleeping bag in a horse stall at rodeos because I couldn't afford a room, and then there have been some of the most glamorous stays one old country boy can imagine." The fortunes of cowboys on the rodeo circuit are always in flux, so they do what they can for their colleagues.

During World Wars I and II, the cowboys who could not volunteer supported the war effort through the promotion of war bonds and the conservation of resources. Today, this spirit can still be seen among competitors at rodeos. Even though cowboys may be competing in the same events, it does not mean that they are only looking out for themselves. In fact, cowboys are always sharing, be it equipment, information about a particular bucking horse or nasty bull, or simply a ride to the next big event; cowboys are the shining example of good sportsmanship. Unlike stars of other sports, cowboys are genuinely approachable. They love to talk to the fans and sign autographs and so are natural ambassadors for their sport. This was not always the case. After all, the reputation of the cowboy was not always so sparkling clean, but today, good behavior and even better manners are the norm.

This good behavior and kindness is also demonstrated by the treatment of animals in the sport. Any cowboy in a rough stock event knows that half of the score comes from the animal and half from the cowboy. If an animal athlete does not perform to its highest capabilities, neither can the cowboy. Riders who draw a less-than-spectacular mount will then have the option of a re-ride; however, that can be a daunting choice fraught with danger. Riders involved in timed events are even more dependent upon their animals for prizes. If a horse is not up to snuff, a cowboy's options are limited; it is hard to compete with an uncooperative animal under you. Therefore, it is logical to assume that riders will take better care of the animals than they do of themselves. This is true both during an animal's days of competition and after they have been retired to pasture. Harry Vold, one of the stock contractors in Colorado, keeps his retired bucking broncs in a nice pasture in Avondale.

Rodeo equipment has been adapted over the years to reflect changing rules. This is modern bareback equipment on a fence at the Evergreen Rodeo in 2003. Early bareback riders would use two hands to hang onto the horse's mane and would have to ride until the horse was exhausted. *Photograph courtesy of Marci Chambers*

Above Trace Axtell looks like he should be fighting super villains instead of busting mutton. Rodeo has become a mix of old and new in the twenty-first century. *Photograph courtesy of Dody Schulze*

Below A saddle bronc rider is pictured just as he is about to kiss the dirt at the 2000 Elizabeth Stampede. A rider must remain on the animal for eight seconds to receive a score. *Photograph courtesy of Steve Diamond*

This bull appears to be flying at the Collegiate Peaks Stampede. Bulls are bred to throw their rider, and it is almost always the rider who gets hurt in this extreme sport. *Photograph courtesy of Rebecca Woolmington*

Below This cowboy holds a cattle prod. These are used to control and direct rodeo animals. Cattle prods deliver a small shock to the animal and are among the many complaints of animal rights groups against the rodeo. *Photograph courtesy of Stephanie Seifried*

Here, opening day ceremonies at the Winter Park-Fraser High Country Stampede and Rodeo on July 5, 2003, are pictured. *Photograph courtesy of Debbie Wolf*

Right This bull fighter appears to be in jeopardy at the Colorado Pro Rodeo Association bull fighting championship in Castle Rock, Colorado, summer 2000. *Photograph courtesy of Becky Pagnotta*

"We like to keep our horses around forever. It's like an old folks home, and it can get costly, but they've earned their keep."

To this end, the PRCA has developed a set of guidelines for the treatment of livestock. This is a set of rules that actually goes back to the 1930s. Today, the PRCA consults with the American Veterinary Medicine Association (AVMA) and accepts its recommendations for the care of rodeo animals. Spectators at PRCA events should be aware that all animals in the arena are treated in the most humane manner since all card-carrying PRCA members are obligated to follow all sixty rules dealing with livestock treatment. PRCA rodeos also have a veterinarian on the site at all times in case of an injury. When an injury does occur, procedures are in place to take care of the animal. When an animal goes down, a set of screens is immediately brought out to help block the audience from the horse's or cattle's vision. The injured animal is then removed from the ring on a stretcher that is attached to a trailer. A veterinarian assumes care of the animal and determines the best course of action for the animal's well-being and health. On occasion, an animal unfortunately has to be put down, but this is an exceedingly rare occurrence.

Smaller rodeos may have a different set of rules, but the PRCA holds many conferences for smaller rodeo groups to educate them about the proper treatment of rodeo animals. Those within the PRCA who break the rules are disqualified and fined. The PRCA is dedicated to ensuring the safety and well-being of its livestock. The responsibility for evaluating the livestock falls on the judges, who are trained not only to judge the performance of cowboys, but also to notice any problems with the animals during the competition. "If a guy uses unnecessary roughness when flanking his calf, he's automatically fined and disqualified," according to the PRCA rules. These judges are put through rigorous training both in, and in some cases, outside of the ring. They are required to continue training throughout the course of their careers.

One could argue that the animals are treated better than the cowboys who ride them. The injury rate for animals in the sixty-seven PRCA-sanctioned rodeos held throughout the year is very low. "Of the 85,638 animal exposures, 25 were injured.... [T]hat translates into a rate of less than three-hundredths of one percent." Some critics will point to the flank straps used on bucking stock as an example of cruelty to animals, but those who have spent time researching what makes an animal buck, e.g. stock contractors, will tell you that a majority of animals will not buck. Breeders are looking for traits such as muscular hindquarters. In other words, animals have to be bred to buck. A flank strap tied too tightly to the animal will usually prevent the animal from bucking, an undesirable occurrence. The purpose of the strap is to cause the horse or bull to want to rid itself of the object by bucking, not to prevent that action. A horse has eighteen ribs to protect its kidney, and the flank strap is placed so that its organs are in no danger. Despite a popular misconception, the strap is not placed near the animal's genital area. Flank straps also do not have any foreign objects protruding from the strap into the animal to cause pain as this is against PRCA rules. To prevent injury or discomfort to the animal, flank straps must be lined with sheepskin or neoprene. Most cowboys respect the bucking animals, and, usually, they are the ones who pay the price with their own bodies for having quality animals in the arena.

As for calves and steers, they must meet certain requirements. Calves used in roping events must be in good health and weigh 220–280 pounds. These animals grow so fast that they will only appear in a few rodeos before they are too large to compete. Steers used in team roping must weigh less than 650 pounds while the steers used in the bulldogging events must meet a minimum weight requirement of 450 pounds, which is a lot heavier than the guy attempting to catch and control the steer. If anyone is going to be hurt in steer wrestling, it will most likely be the cowboy. While the horns of the animal are covered to protect man and beast, injuries still occur. In steer wrestling, the rate of injury for the cowboy is 8.7 percent, according to the *Denver Post* in 2003. This is quite a bit better than the bull riders, who also get up close and personal with a bovine.

Another complaint of those who oppose rodeo is the use of cattle prods, which are powered by flashlight batteries, and the use of spurs in competition. The PRCA rules state that the prod should be used as little as possible and only used on the shoulder or hip area. Dr. Jeff Hall, who has spent many years working with cattle, does not feel a prod is harmful. "I personally have been shocked with the type of device on several occasions. This type of shock was annoying but produced no lasting or harmful effects." Spurs, which are worn by cowboys on the heels of their boots, are dulled to avoid injury to the animal. In fact, the PRCA has stated since 1938 that locked rowels may not be used and that spurs must be less than one eighth of an inch thick. Both of these measures prevent the spurs from tearing into the animals, which have skin that is five to seven times thicker than human skin. Both timed and rough stock contestants try to improve performance by using spurs, but not to harm the animal.

Rodeo has always had a bit of a problem with animal rights groups,

Cowboys are used to working together and helping one another. Here, a hazer aids a bulldogger at the 2001 Elizabeth Stampede. A hazer usually receives 25 percent of the winnings. *Photograph courtesy of Maria Armstrong*

Below The main drag of Deer Trail, Colorado, is pictured. While famous for the first rodeo in Colorado, today it is also the home of an annual rodeo known as the Deer Trail Rodeo. *Photograph by Dino G. Maniatis*

The Professional Rodeo Cowboys Association has strict rules regarding spurs. They can only be an eighth of an inch thick, and they cannot have locking rowels. These spurs were photographed at the 2003 National Western Stock Show Rodeo. *Photograph courtesy of Maria Armstrong*

going back to almost the very beginning of the sport. Today, one of the biggest rodeo opponents is People for the Ethical Treatment of Animals (PETA). This group is dedicated to animal rights and advocates vegetarianism. PETA is also against the wearing of animal skins of all types, including leather and especially fur, which its members have been known to splash with gallons of red paint. Currently, PETA is engaged in a "Buck the Rodeo" campaign, and produced quite a bit of literature. The group is lobbying the governor of Wyoming to remove the rodeo imagery from its license plates, writing letters such as the following:

> I am writing on behalf of People for the Ethical Treatment of Animals' more than 600,000 members to ask that you modernize your state's "bucking bronco" license plate to reflect twenty-first century understanding of the nature of animals…. We hope Wyoming will give the "bucking bronco" license plate the boot.

This letter goes on to argue the organization's position on rodeo and present its evidence of cruelty in rodeos. PETA's Web site maintains a list of "animals injured or killed in rodeos." However, of the forty-seven incidents listed from 1995 to January 2004, several involved injuries to people, not animals, and a few others described no injuries at all. Statistics compiled by the PRCA show very few animals being injured in the course of rodeo.

PETA has also lobbied the PRCA to curtail the use of flank straps in rodeo and to eliminate the calf roping events altogether. The following letter to PRCA president Steven Hatchell presents its concerns:

> The rodeo is not a sport; it is a macho bully fest. Please consider that the horses and bulls used during the events buck violently and beyond their normal ability because of the straps and ropes cinched tightly around their abdomen…. During calf roping, calves, running at speeds of up to 27 miles per hour, are jerked off their feet by a rope slung around their necks and then slammed to the ground.

What this organization overlooks is that these skills were needed in the Old West to protect animals. A calf would have been roped if it needed medical attention. This was the only way to help this animal on the open range. Steer roping would have been performed for similar reasons. PETA also tends to overlook the injuries incurred by human competitors in rodeo, which are more common and more severe than the few injuries sustained by livestock. Its members are so dedicated to the cause of animal rights in rodeo

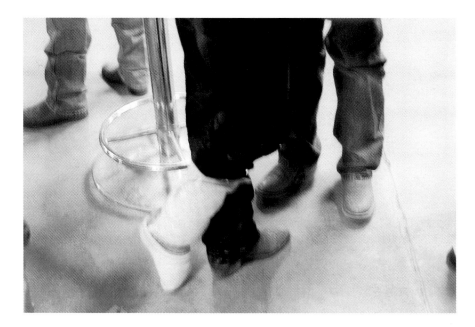

A cowboy ices his ankle before the night's competition. Rodeo injuries are common, and most cowboys do not have health insurance. Many rely on the donation of services by groups such as HealthSouth and Justin Sports Medicine. *Photograph by the author*

that they were seen handing out pamphlets at the 2004 National Western Stock Show in Denver, which would have been a tough crowd to convince.

A section of PETA's Web site is dedicated to encouraging its members to write and e-mail rodeo sponsors from Dodge Trucks to Coors Brewing Company. The goal is to discourage these large corporations from making contributions to the sport. PETA is overlooking the fact that, with over seventy stock contractors throughout the country, competition can be fierce for the best and healthiest stock. These are valuable animals, and once they are done bucking and their rodeo careers are over, the animals can still produce profit by breeding, making them unlikely candidates for the slaughterhouse. The science of animal husbandry is very exacting, and a proven bucker can sire many offspring, making quite a bit of money for its owner. Economic considerations aside, PETA is a determined group, but history has shown that rodeo is a tough survivor of many different animal rights protests. Today, rodeo is a way of life for many and an exciting event for those who lack the daring to actually try to ride a bull themselves. Rodeo is a sport that is growing and becoming more and more popular, due in part to television. From its beginnings in the nineteenth century, rodeo has only seen its numbers go up. In 2001, more fans attended rodeos than in any other year in the history of the sport.

This is a sport that is very accessible to the novice because of the efforts of talented rodeo announcers throughout the country. Part entertainers and part educators, announcers must let the rookie spectators know what is going on and why while simultaneously providing the information needed for

This bull has had its horns dulled for the protection of bull riders, who are in danger of being gored once they have been thrown from the animal. *Photograph by Stephanie Seifried*

Below Horses and bulls wait for a chance to throw a cowboy or cowgirl into the air at the Jefferson County Fair Grounds. Odds are the cowboys will suffer more injuries than these animals. *Photograph by Stephanie Seifried*

Facing page Animals are important in rodeo. This photo shows a man and a boy taking care of their horse at the World Arena in Colorado Springs, Colorado. *Photograph courtesy of Meredith Smart*

Right A rodeo announcer has the job of educating first-time rodeo-goers, keeping rodeo enthusiasts informed, and entertaining the crowd during breaks in the action. *Photograph by the author*

Below This horse is sporting an elaborate hairstyle at the 2003 Meeker Range Call and Rodeo. Even horses need to look good before competition. *Photograph courtesy of Sharon Bradshaw*

those who eat, sleep, and breathe rodeo. They also interact with the rodeo clowns during breaks in the action, keeping an audience's attention from wandering. An announcer must have a quick eye and a silver tongue to be successful. Just like cowboys, announcers are also honored at the Hall of Fame, as are bull fighters, trick riders, and those behind the scenes dealing with the more mundane aspects of the sport such as record-keeping.

Records are rodeo's lifelines. Without someone keeping track of the information, rodeo would be lost. Someone must record the scores and times, someone must hand out the checks, and someone must report the results to the organization sanctioning the event, be it the Little Britches Rodeo or the PRCA. Secretaries are the heart and soul of any organization, and they are often overlooked, as are those behind the chutes taking care of the animals and preparing them for their big moment. Many hours go into producing any rodeo, from the weekend affairs in the mountains to the Colorado State Fair. Rodeo is a lot of work for all involved, but it is also a way of life that has overcome many obstacles to become the major sport it is today. This is a sport that only promises to get bigger as more and more Americans discover their pasts in rodeo rings throughout the country.

CONCLUSION

ODEO IS THE ONLY SPORT that developed from a profession, and it has developed into something very similar yet very different from what it began as in the 1800s. Today, this sport is a huge industry, with professions ranging from livestock contractors to those who manufacture the equipment needed by cowboys. Why is rodeo so popular today? The answer is simple. The sport of rodeo reminds us of our past. We as Americans have a sense of nostalgia for our frontier roots, especially those in the West. Americans are identified as cowboys by the rest of the world, sometimes in a positive manner, sometimes in a negative manner. Regardless of the connotations, there is no evading this cowboy image of our country and our people. We wear cowboy hats at the Olympics, our president meets with world champion cowboys, and we cannot escape our past, especially if we continue to embrace it with such affection.

Author Louis L'Amour has written many novels on the way the West was. Even if his stories are not quite as accurate as history, they are part of our culture and have become part of our history in their own unique way. With his novels of the Sackett family and with L'Amour's own lifestyle of spending his days in the Strater Hotel and the Diamond Belle Saloon in Durango, he has created an image that is hard to ignore. This image is so hard to ignore that it has become accepted as truth in the hearts of many Americans. Today, Hollywood continues to produce films based on what we believe to be the authentic history of the Old West, some of them coming from L'Amour's own novels. The John Wayne film *Hondo* was based on the story *The Gift of Cochise*. These novels and stories may not be historically accurate; however, it is this sense of romance and adventure that keeps us coming back for more. We love the danger; we love the idea of the lone cowboy who saves the day and gets the girl just in time to ride off into the sunset.

A hoof print in the mud framed by tire tracks is a fitting symbol of the modern sport of rodeo where cowboys travel by truck to get thrown from horses and bulls in towns and cities throughout the country. *Photograph by Stephanie Seifried*

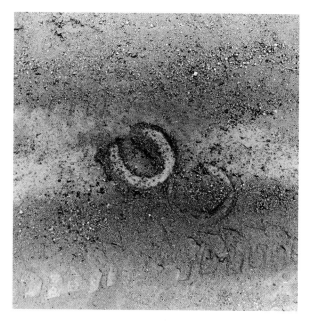

Above left A bull rider stretches before tangling with a 1,600-pound animal at the 2004 National Western Stock Show. More cowboys are training for the sport, but it is still a slow transition to modern athletic training techniques. *Photograph by Mathew Staver*

Above right Rodeo is a way of preserving the past. Here, a man drives a team of six horses around the Denver Coliseum showing off a skill that is quickly dying in our modern society. *Photograph by the author*

Left While rodeo is a sport that is gaining in popularity, you wouldn't be able to tell from this turnout for a high school rodeo on a snowy morning. *Photograph courtesy of Stephanie Seifried*

Below Team #6 at a rodeo in Grover, Colorado, works to get a horse under control for a wild horse race. This would have been useful on the range when attempting to capture and tame wild horses to use while herding cattle. *Photograph courtesy of Kirk Rush*

A lone cowboy sits in the mud changing into his boots in preparation for his chance to ride. A protective vest hangs on the fence to the left. *Photograph courtesy of Stephanie Seifried*

Below This cowboy is practicing the art of calf roping. Although this is a skill that is no longer needed by most of us to survive, we still embrace our past through rodeos such as this one held near Colorado Springs in 2000. *Photograph courtesy of Stephen Zacker*

Even though this cowboy can't walk, he is already becoming immersed in the sport at the WDS Junior Rodeo in Eaton, Colorado. *Photograph courtesy of Emily Beaton*

Lee Rush rides an ostrich at the Strasburg Hometown Days in July of 1999, showing rodeo isn't just about steers and horses.
Photograph courtesy of Kirk Rush

Below Rodeo is an American sport and is often scheduled around the Fourth of July holiday, celebrating the independence of our country. Rodeos such as the High Country Stampede Rodeo in Fraser, Colorado, in 2003, follow this proud tradition.
Photograph courtesy of Cathy A. Weninger

Above Real cowboys and cowgirls don't mind mud. In fact, they get used to it at a young age as the Anderson siblings prove at the 2003 Larimer County Fair and Rodeo.
Photograph courtesy of Kim Anderson

This bull rider's chaps are not quite as lucky as he thought. The unfortunate four-leaf-clover wearer is about to eat dust. *Photograph courtesy of Glen Bishard*

We love to sit spellbound on the edge of our seats as these men and women risk danger, which explains why rodeo is still going strong as it moves into its third century of existence. "It was fun, but you have to be a little bit wild…. It is an exciting life, and I wouldn't trade my rodeo for anything," a former bareback rider relates, which seems to sum up the sport quite nicely. Rodeo is a fun, wild, and exciting lifestyle.

Rodeo is a sport that is driven by adrenaline. Cowboys can go from the top of the world one minute to lying in the dirt with both their dreams and their bodies crushed beneath the hoof of an indifferent animal the next minute. Cowboys go from living the high life in one city to sleeping in the stable with their horse two cities later. Both the sport and the lifestyle are roller-coaster rides that are not for the faint of heart. This is a sport that has been quietly gaining ground for years. These men and women may only work a

Above left Bull rider Rob Watton hangs on tight at the Labor Day Rodeo in Trinidad, Colorado, in 2000. Bull riders are taking rodeo to a whole new generation via cable and network television. *Photograph courtesy of Bernadette Dickinson*

Above right Cowboys are a tough group. This group waits out the rainstorm at the Douglas County/Elbert County Ranch Rodeo in Kiowa, Colorado, in 2003. *Photograph courtesy of Lori Ellefson*

Left Jerod Ashen attempts to tackle and milk a wild cow in 2003 without a lot of success. Rodeo is more than just the five major events. Many rodeos also have a few special events to keep things even more interesting. *Photograph courtesy of Terry White*

Below A decrepit gas station in Deer Trail, Colorado, sits on the site of the first rodeo in Colorado between cowboys of rival cattle ranches. The winner received a suit of clothes. *Photograph by Dino G. Maniatis*

Top left This little cowboy is eager to join in the fun of rodeo as he stands near the bucking chutes at the Rollin' H Arena in Brush, Colorado, 2003. *Photograph courtesy of Sandy Kane*

Top right Respect for animals is one of the major themes of rodeo. Animals were more important than the cowboy in most cases in the Old West. *Photograph courtesy of Therese Mousel*

Bottom left These cowboys sort their gear in the mud at the Jefferson County Fair Grounds on a snowy April morning. *Photograph courtesy of Stephanie Seifried*

Bottom right A muddy rider works to recapture a bucking bronc at a high school rodeo in April 2004. *Photograph courtesy of Stephanie Seifried*

few minutes a year, but when they do work, they work hard. It is no simple task to rope a calf or to ride a bull. No one could argue the fact that rodeo cowboys earn their money the hard way, the same way that the earliest rodeo cowboys earned their money.

In the early years, cowboys may not have always been the most respectable folks; in fact, they were infamous for causing trouble when in the big cities. But today, they have done an about-face. In a 1954 letter to the editor of the *Rodeo Sports News,* Patty Ols of Knox, Indiana, writes, "I want to go on the record as saying I have never in my life met anyone so kind and considerate as the boys and girls in rodeo." Today, rodeo is full of some of the nicest professional athletes you will ever meet, and they are professionals, not prima donnas. Anyone accusing these men and women of this obviously knows very little of the sport. Cowboys will help out a fellow cowboy in need, which

seems to be good policy based on the simple principle of karma. After all, you never know when you will be the one who needs a helping hand. Cowboys have also learned the art of good sportsmanship. Cowboys frequently carpool, and you never want to be the loser riding with a winner who will not stop gloating. Therefore, cowboys learned long ago you don't rub in the fact that you won, and they pass that tradition on to their children along with the rest of the traditions of the sport.

Rodeo is both a sport and a culture; it is also becoming one of the fastest growing sports in America with many different levels of competition ranging from the three-year-old mutton buster to the high school student who competes on weekends to the professional with millions of dollars in endorsements. This is no small feat for something that was considered a job not so long ago; in fact, the rise of rodeo in the United States and in Colorado is a wonderful thing. It allows the old rodeo families to keep their traditions while inviting those who can't tell a bull from a steer to remember where they really came from and to embrace the Wild West past of this great country.

Above left This rodeo clown takes a moment for reflection at the Collegiate Peaks Stampede Rodeo in Buena Vista, Colorado, July 2003. *Photograph courtesy of Kelly Doke*

Above right Bill Schulze and Todd Axtell wait their turn in the team roping event at the Granby Rodeo in July 2002. It appears they are ready to ride off into the sunset like a couple of Hollywood cowboys who have saved the day. *Photograph courtesy of Dody Schulze*

Rodeo is a family affair, and, often, children follow parents on the rodeo circuit before joining the circuit themselves. *Photograph courtesy of Therese Mousel*

BIBLIOGRAPHY

ARCHIVAL MATERIALS

Little Britches Rodeo Program, 1958.

Pikes Peak or Bust Rodeo Program, 1955.

Pro Rodeo Cowboy Association Definitions Handout.

Rodeo Tally Book of Contestants and Rodeo Records, 1957.

Spanish Trails Fiesta Pamphlet Published by San Juan Basin Rodeo
	Association, 1941.

Spanish Trails Fiesta Pamphlet Published by San Juan Basin Rodeo
	Association, 1946.

Stout, Dave. "History of the U.S. Rodeo." Archives of Colorado Springs
	Pro Rodeo Museum and Hall of Fame, 1978.

Westermier, Clifford P. "Man, Beast, Dust: The Story of Rodeo." Ph.D. diss.,
	University of Colorado, 1947.

BOOKS

Emrich, David. *Hollywood, Colorado: the Selig Polyscope Company and the Colorado
	Motion Picture Company.* Lakewood, Colo.: Post Modern Co., 1997.

Fredriksson, Kristine. *American Rodeo: from Buffalo Bill to Big Business.* College
	Station: Texas A&M University Press, 1983.

Gibson, Barbara. *The Lower Downtown Historic District.* Denver, Colo.:
	Historic Denver Inc., 1995.

Iverson, Peter. *Riders of the West: Portraits from Indian Rodeo.* Seattle: Greystone
	Books, University of Washington Press, 1999.

Lawrence, Elizabeth Atwood. *Rodeo, An Anthropologist Looks at the Wild and the
	Tame.* Chicago: University of Chicago Press, 1982.

Weston, Jack. *The Real American Cowboy.* New York: Schocken Books, 1985.

"Buck the Rodeo." *People for the Ethical Treatment of Animals.*
    <http://www.bucktherodeo.com> (12 February 2004).

"Colorado Junior Rodeo Association." <http://www.coloradojrrodeo.com/
    aboutus.htm> (22 February 2004).

"Colorado State High School Rodeo Association." <http://www.cshsra.org/
    cshsra_mainpage.htm> (24 September 2003).

Garcia, Socorro; Ramon Gomez; and Desiree Crawford. "Black Cowboys
    Rode the Trails, Too." *Borderlands: An El Paso Community College Local
    History Project.* <http://www.epcc.edu/ftp/Homes/monicaw/borderlands/
    21_black_cowboys.htm> (26 September 2003).

Harwitz, Paul. "Bill Pickett (1870–1932) Rodeo Star." <http://www.coax.net/
    people/lwf/pickett.htm> (26 September 2003).

"Little Britches Rodeo." *National Little Britches Rodeo Association.*
    <http://www.nlbra.org> (20 January 2004).

"Mike 'The Business Man' Cervi." *Cervi Championship Rodeo Company.*
    <http://cervirodeo.com/Founder.html> (1 March 2004).

"National Intercollegiate Rodeo Association." <http://www.collegerodeo.com/
    history.shtml> (22 September 2003).

"O'Farrell Hatmakers of Durango." <http://www.ofarrellhats.com> (9 March
    2004).

"Old Pueblo Saddle Company." <http://www.oldpueblosaddle.com/
    saddlemaker.html> (10 March 2004).

"PRCA Animal Welfare Rules." *Professional Rodeo Cowboys Association.*
    <http://www.prorodeo.org/animals/rules.html> (4 February 2003).

Sigmon, Kristie. "Buck the Rodeo: Letter to Governor Jim Geringer."
    People for the Ethical Treatment of Animals. <http://www.bucktherodeo.com/
    platelet.html> (11 March 2004).

"Ty Murray—King of the Cowboys." <http://www.tymurray.com>
    (22 September 2003).

"VisitGunnison.Com." <http://www.visitgunnison.com/navigate.cfm?nav
    =business.cfm> (15 September 2003).

"Westernaires." <http://www.westernaires.org/index.html> (1 March 2004).

"Women's Rodeo History." *Women's Professional Rodeo Association.*
    <http://www.wpra.com/rodeohistory.htm> (23 January 2004).

"Working Ranch Cowboys Association." <http://www.wrca.org> (9 March
    2004).

INTERVIEWS

Bashline, Tom; Valley Rodeo Club Sponsor. Interview by author.
    22 February 2004.

Cundiff, Brenda; Basin Rodeo Club Sponsor. Interview by author.
    19 February 2004.

Elliot, Guy; National Western Stock Show Manager, 1982–2001. Interview
    by author. 27 August 2003.

Sear, Jay; Lazy Lopers Member. Interview by author. 8 March 2004.

Vason, Lu; Producer of the Bill Pickett Rodeo, 1984–Present. Interview by
    author. 13 January 2004.

MAGAZINES

Bwaltmy, Bill. "Invisible Hero: The Image and the Reality of the Black
    Cowboy." *Footsteps: African American Heritage,* March/April 1999.

Daye, Melanie. "Bruce Ford, A Living Legend." *Colorado Country Life,*
    January 2002.

"Ranchers Rodeo." *Colorado Country Life,* June 2003.

Scher, Zeke. "Tribute to Midnight from 1930s Rodeo." *Denver Post Magazine,*
    9 January 1983.

NEWSPAPERS

Colorado Springs Gazette, 24 June 1951.

Craig (Colo.) Daily Press, 17 January 1974.

Denver Daily Record Stockman, 19 January 1931.

Denver Monitor, 21 December 1951.

Denver News, January 1952, 22 January 1954, 16 January 1963.

Denver Post, 9 January 1931, 17–20 January 1931, 22 January 1931,
    24 January 1931, 10 January 1932, 21 January 1932, 24 January 1932,
    7 January 1942, 14 January 1946, 10 January 1952, 19 January 1952,
    January 1958, 16 April 1961, 18 January 1968, 23 April 1972,
    22 August 1976, 12 January 1983, 11 January 1995, 10 January 2003,
    7–8 December 2003.

Field and Farm, 8 July 1889.

Grand Junction (Colo.) Sentinel, 27 November 1981, 9 January 1985.

Greeley (Colo.) Tribune, 14 January 1961.

Kiowa County (Colo.) Press, 2 June 1939.

Loveland (Colo.) Reporter-Herald, 29 April 1946, 10 January 1968.

New York Times News Service, 23 August 2003.

Omaha Journal, 7 January 1931.

Pueblo Colorado Star-Journal and Sunday Chieftain, 19 October 1969, 26 October
     1969.

Record Stockman, January 1943.

Rocky Mountain News, 1 January 1931, 17 January 1931, 22 January 1931,
     24–25 January 1931, 12 January 1947, 8 August 1949, 16 January 1957,
     17 January 1960, 27 November 1972, January 1974, 24 December 1979,
     17 January 1986, 10 January 1990, 9 September 1990, 19 August 1993,
     2 January 1995, 9–10 January 2004.

Rodeo Sports News (Colorado Springs), 1 December 1954.

Steamboat Pilot, 21 June 2003.

MISCELLANEOUS

Animal Welfare: The Care and Treatment of Professional Rodeo Livestock. Professional
     Rodeo Cowboys Association.

Carey, Rita, comp. The Greeley Independence Stampede: Celebrating 75 Years of
     Tradition. Greeley, Colo.: Greeley Independence Stampede, 1996.

Deer Trail Historic Marker of the First Rodeo.

The Sport of Cowboys: An Inside Look into the World of the Professional Rodeo.
     Professional Rodeo Cowboys Association Pamphlet.